S0-BZJ-635

A Society in Peril

Edited by
Kevin Perrotta and John C. Blattner

A Pastoral Renewal Book

SERVANT BOOKS
Ann Arbor, Michigan

Pastoral Renewal books are published by
Servant Books in cooperation with
the Center for Pastoral Renewal.

Copyright © 1989 The Center for Pastoral Renewal
All rights reserved.

Published by Servant Books
P.O. Box 8617
Ann Arbor, Michigan 48107

89 90 91 92 93 10 9 8 7 6 5 4 3 2 1
Printed in the United States of America
ISBN 0-89283-636-9

Contents

Contributors

William B. Ball, a constitutional attorney specializing in the litigation of religious liberties cases, is a partner in Ball, Skelly, Murren & Connell, in Harrisburg, Pennsylvania.

John C. Blattner is the executive director of the Center for Pastoral Renewal.

Francis Canavan is a Jesuit priest and professor of political science at Fordham University in New York.

Stanley S. Harakas is professor of Orthodox Christian ethics at Holy Cross Greek Orthodox School of Theology in Brookline, Massachusetts.

William E. May is professor of moral theology at the Catholic University of America.

Marvin Olasky is professor of journalism at the University of Texas in Austin.

J.I. Packer is professor of historical and systematic theology at Regent College in Vancouver, British Columbia.

Janet E. Smith is an associate professor in the department of liberal studies at the University of Notre Dame.

John H. White is vice-president for religious services at Geneva College, in Beaver Falls, Pennsylvania, and president of the National Association of Evangelicals.

Paul C. Vitz is professor of psychology at New York University.

Introduction

THE PRESENT BOOK IS THE FRUIT of a meeting of Christian leaders who gathered at Wheaton College in June 1988 to confront the roots of decay in American society and in the churches, and to search out avenues for renewal. Under the banner of "A Society in Peril," speaker Charles Colson, the contributors to this volume, and several others offered their analyses of problems and insights into effective responses. The gist of their deliberations is that there are no easy formulas—certainly no political formulas—for solving the problems we face, and that fundamental solutions will only come to light as Christians repent of their acceptance of non-Christian values and habits and renew their faithfulness to Christ and his word.

Drawing together an unusually wide variety of Christian leaders, "A Society in Peril" was the latest of a series of conferences entitled "Allies for Faith and Renewal." A word about these "Allies" conferences will help to explain the nature and purpose of the present book.

At the start of the 1980s the Center for Pastoral Renewal, in Ann Arbor, Michigan, began inviting scholars, pastoral leaders, and activists from Protestant, Roman Catholic, and Orthodox churches to examine the conflicts between Christianity and contemporary culture. While virtually all Christian communions suffer the corrosive effects of contemporary intellectual and cultural trends, from antisupernaturalism in theology to materialism and hedonism in daily life, opportunities are few for Christian leaders from across the great church divides to gather in the Lord's presence and seek wisdom together about dealing with these developments. The Center is an outreach of an interconfessional community, The Sword of the Spirit, which is marked by ecumenical cooperation and a focus on Christian experience and everyday life. Thus it hoped to provide a meeting ground for Christians of different traditions to gather who are seeking to respond to the urgent theological, pastoral, and spiritual challenges of the day within the framework of historic biblical, trinitarian Christianity.

The initial meetings proved successful, and "Allies" conferences now take place annually, with about 350 to 400 participants. The results have been published in several volumes: *Christianity Confronts Modernity, Summons to Faith and Renewal, Christianity in Conflict, Courage in Leadership,* and *Christian Allies in a Secular Age (*all published by Servant Books and available through the Center for Pastoral Renewal: see page 165).

The present volume follows these earlier books, with one differ-ence. Unlike earlier Allies conferences, the 1988 conference, in addition to varied contributions by several speakers, featured a series of lectures by a single speaker, Charles Colson, the founder of Prison Fellowship Ministries. Because of the substantial nature of Mr. Colson's lecture series, his presentations are being published in a separate book, *Against the Night* (also from Servant Books). The present volume is like its predecessors, however, in that the contributors deal with a wide range of issues, as part of a joint reconnaisance of challenges facing all Christians in contemporary society.

Charles Colson's Message

The authors of the chapters of this book expand on aspects of the social and church situations that Charles Colson broached in his lectures. In order to see the unity of the book, then, it is helpful to have some idea of the burden of Charles Colson's lectures. His argument may be summarized as follows.

We now face a crisis in Western culture greater than any since the barbarian invasions that overthrew the Roman empire in the West and almost extinguished civilization from the fourth to the tenth centuries. This time, however, the "barbarians" are not unlettered men who destroy cultural institutions from the outside. Rather they are sophisticated but unprincipled men and women who disdain the moral heritage of Western civilization and whose ideas, therefore, are socially destructive.

This new barbarism can be traced to the eighteenth-century Enlightenment's loosing of morality from its religious moorings, from its foundation in transcendent truth. The eventual outcome of this loss of moral anchorage has been a reduced sense of moral obligation. As morality has been relativized, the communities and institutions that help individuals recognize their moral obligations to one another have declined, and Individualism has become ascendent. Truth with a transcendent religious base has been forced out of public life; for example, the truth of the sanctity of human life is rejected, and abortion, infanticide, and euthanasia gain acceptance.

But "societies depend on individuals who will act on the basis of motives superior to their immediate interest." Where self-interest reigns, human character is destroyed, and every human institution is undermined. The *family* disintegrates, and fails to play its role of civilizing the next generation. The consequences in the moral impoverishment of the young become apparent in the rise of crime, sexual promiscuity, and other disorders. Under the influence of the "new barbarism," *schools* no longer provide character formation. *Politics* becomes a naked war of interest against interest, unrestrained by commitment to the common good. *Churches,* marginalized by the rejection of religion, normative truth, and moral absolutes in public life, concern themselves with a privatized religion, a gospel of good feelings, focused on the self.

How can a return to social harmony and well-being be found? A decade ago some theologically conservative Christians hoped that a reversal in political policies would spearhead social restoration. But ten years after the rise of the New Christian Right, the "sun is setting on the hopes of once euphoric Christians" that politics can succeed in getting at the problems. It is now clearer than ever that only the churches can lead a "reform of manners." This is so because only the churches have an independent authority, an independent standard, a place from which to stand and speak to society. With the authority of the Bible, the revealed word of God, and in the power of the Holy Spirit the churches can "take a stand as the main line of resistance against the new barbarians, providing culture with a new sense of moral vision."

In order to do this, however, the churches must model what they call society to. They must first demonstrate what they preach about how human life should be lived. They must be faithful to their identity as the body of Christ. Thus, paradoxically, in order to fulfill their role in regard to the larger culture, the churches must set as their first goal not the performing of one or another particular service to society but simple faithfulness to Christ and obedience to his ways. A historical parallel for the churches' mission in our own day may be found in the rise of monastic communities in Western Europe in the aftermath of the collapse of Roman civilization. Christian men and women founded these communities not with a view to transforming culture but in the desire to seek God above all and to live the Christian life together. But as the monastic communities modeled the Christian life, they became sowers of the seeds of a new Christian civilization.

Thus the priorities for Christians today are not in the field of political action, although this has its importance, but in repentance, in taking a stand on biblical revelation and the historical confessions of Christian truth, and in living the life of the holy community, so that Christ's light might shine even in the darkest circumstances. "In the midst of chaos, the church's fundamental responsibility is to renew its own integrity and to be a repentant community."

As the churches respond to the Lord's call to renew their identity in him, they will then be able to hold the culture to moral judgment, show it the way back to eternal things, restore its language of moral discourse, and provide it with living examples of an other-directed, rather than self-directed, way of life. Renewed churches will support family life, the fundamental workshop of personal formation in moral virtue. Whether, by responding to this call, the churches will open the way for a fundamental renewal of Western society is not something we can know. It is conceivable that Western civilization has passed the point of no return. In any case, the renewal of the entire social order is not the basic reason for our response. Our actions are motivated by the desire to please our gracious Lord, come what may. In responding to him, even in the grimmest hour, we may have the hope and joy that accompany obedience and faith.

Diagnoses and Responses

Other conference speakers developed points raised by Mr. Colson. William B. Ball, the noted constitutional attorney, examined how the courts have closed themselves to the law's grounding in the Western moral heritage, and have settled for a materialistic utilitarianism that gives short shrift to religious liberty and the sanctity of human life.

Marvin Olasky, a journalist and professor of journalism, illustrated the "new barbarism" in the press, which is largely closed to the spiritual dimension of human life and renders both God's providence and human sin invisible, promoting the view that all solutions are to be sought in the perfection of human institutions. Francis Canavan, a political scientist, explored the partnership between extreme individualism and state power that is eroding the integrity of family life and the life of religious institutions.

The assault on the Christian moral heritage within the churches themselves came under careful examination by the prominent evangelical theologian J.I. Packer. Dr. Packer sketched the basic structure of biblical morality and identified the key principles underlying contemporary departures from it. Thus he attempted to mark out the common ground where Protestants, Roman Catholics, and Orthodox may take a stand together against contemporary attempts to overturn historic, biblical positions in moral teaching. Two speakers offered prepared responses to Dr. Packer's analysis: Stanley S. Harakas, a Greek Orthodox ethicist, and William E. May, a Roman Catholic moral theologian, each arguably the foremost scholar in his field in the United States.

Not content to diagnose problems, speakers pointed to positive responses. University of Notre Dame scholar Janet E. Smith argued that now is a time to present the Christian view of sexuality with particular confidence, and drew on her own experience in the university and in the prolife movement to illustrate how Christian apologetics for biblical morality can be presented most effectively. Reformed theologian John H. White, president of the National Association of Evangelicals, drew on biblical texts and the historic experiences of Catholic and Protestant renewal movements to mark out a path for Christian social engagement that avoids the pitfalls of either accommodation to non-Christian values or flight from social responsibilities. Paul Vitz, a professor of psychology, provided useful insight into the evangelistic terrain on which Christians must fight, by exposing the psychological underpinnings of many modern people's reluctance to believe in God. John C. Blattner, director of the Center for Pastoral Renewal and conference chairman, described an approach to personal pastoral care that helps Christians overcome the erosion of Christian character.

The presentations published in this book, as well as others that could not be included,[8] including those of Charles Colson, are

available on audio tape from the Center for Pastoral Renewal.*
Further information about this can be found on page 165. The reader
will also find there information about future Allies for Faith and
Renewal conferences, which are open to any Christians who wish to
join in the purposes of these conferences, as expressed in the
statement beginning on the next page.

The editors offer the present book in the hope not only that it will
inform Christians throughout the churches of the challenges we face
in common and point the way to authentic Christian responses, but
that it will also inspire readers to turn to God, from whom all
attempts at renewal must flow and from whom all help may be
expected.

John C. Blattner and Kevin Perrotta

---

*These were James Hitchcock, "Christians in America: A People Set Apart?"; Josef
Tson, "The Gospel's Advance through Costly Witness"; Richard Land, "The
Secularization of the Churches: Identifying and Reversing the Threat from Within";
Ralph C. Martin, "The Ultimate Peril"; Peter S. Williamson, "Countering a Crisis of
Character: Leading Christian to Maturity."

Statement of Purpose

We are Christians who want to work together for the cause of Christ. We want to see the message and teaching of Christ presented clearly in the churches and to the world and to see individual Christians and the churches renewed in a living relationship with God.

Though we are confident in Christ's lordship, we see that the increasingly de-Christianized societies of the West present a difficult environment for Christian life and mission. Many of the structures of the modern world tend to undermine Christians' ability to maintain their distinctiveness from the secularist cultures they live in.

We believe that Christians must strengthen their relationships with one another in order to better meet these challenges. We recognize the necessity of Christians living by the teaching of Christ—being a holy nation, a people set apart with a godly way of life.

We also observe a widespread secularization of Christian teaching and ministry. In light of this, we see the need for Christians of all confessional traditions to join together to reassert the fundamental elements of the Christian faith we hold in common.

We believe that the Christian people must unite in loyalty to the authority of God's word. Today both faith in God's revelation and obedience to it are being attacked, directly and indirectly, outside and within the churches. This is an assault that all Christians must resist.

As Protestants, Roman Catholics, and Orthodox we recognize one another as brothers and sisters in Christ. Though we are separated by important differences of belief and church order, we are united in our desire to obey one Lord. Many of the theological, pastoral, cultural, and political challenges our respective churches face confront all Western Christians today. Therefore we want to work together for a better understanding of these challenges, fostering communication and supporting one another in our various roles of service to the Christian people.

Desiring to see a renewal of God's life in his people, we know that renewal must begin in our individual lives with repentance from sin, wholehearted commitment to Christ, and reliance on the power of the Holy Spirit. Moreover we pray for God to intervene in all his people's lives, pardoning us, strengthening us, and extending his kingdom through us.

It is our intention to put our commitment to Christ and his cause in the world above everything else. We want to work together to strengthen one another, to defend Christian teaching, and to bring the world to Christ.

Part I

The Challenges We Face

ONE

The Closing of the American Courts

William Bentley Ball

I AM THE RECIPIENT OF A GREAT DEAL of Disaster Mail.

Through having once, in early and impecunious married life, answered an intriguing ad which offered to provide me, free, a publication which promised to tell me how I could make a fortune without trying, I got myself onto mailing lists of all sorts of financial wizards who for decades have kept me supplied with a frightening flow of Disaster Mail. These warn me of impending mass unemployment, post-World-War-I-German-type inflation, wholesale bank failures, universal starvation.

But then also I receive Disaster Mail related to health. This is some of the worst. One of these solicitations asked me a series of questions—point blank, yes or no: Do you interrupt people in the middle of their sentences? My answer: Yes. Do you eat rapidly? Yes! Are you impatient at red traffic lights? Yes! Then, said the text, you are a Type A—which meant I was headed for a cardiac event or a stroke.

A third type of Disaster Mail which I get pertains to things social and political. The Left Wing Disaster Mail tells me, of course, that nuclear incineration is promised me if fascist storm troopers don't get me first. A bit of the mail from the Right I can equally disregard—for

19

example, that which warns that the Soviets are lacing our beer with minute quantities of strychnine.

The Disaster Mail represents many things. Profit-making—the exploitation of fear for financial gain—is obviously a partial explanation of its volume. But the solicitations apparently pay off, and that is because they not only excite fears; they correspond with fears already active or latent in great numbers of our people. God has permitted us to live in the United States where today so many have the feeling that we are on the edge of some sort of vortex which will presently twirl us down into oblivion. The author Jean Didion, in an interview some years ago, when asked what her most constant sentiment was, responded that it was simply *dread*.

I have approached my assigned subject today through the doorway of a mention of fear, because the title of my talk, "The Closing of the American Courts," is one which may well signal fear to those who hear it. The closing of the American courts, like the closing of the American mind, as described by Alan Bloom, would be a troublesome thing to contemplate. The justice of the jungle, the rule of the violent or powerful, the successes of cheats and panderers—and chaos generally—would be the result. But I think it is useful to examine the subject as one would examine a festering wound—not with the morbidity of fatalists but with the hopefulness of Christians. Let me therefore speak of the closing of the American courts and the opening up of avenues of hope.

Alan Bloom's *Closing of the American Mind* did not tell us that the minds of Americans had now shut down and become inoperative. Rather, its point was that American minds had become narrow, seeking the lowest and rejecting the highest in thought and culture. Similarly, in speaking of the closing of the American courts, I do not suggest that our courts are about to shut down (or that our judges are about to shut up), but rather that they seem to be undergoing a narrowing process in which they, too, are gravitating toward the lowest and tending away from the highest.

The Source of Rights

As I approach this subject, I think it important that I pause a moment to talk about "liberalism" and "conservatism," because those terms, of such varied meanings, are bound to intrude themselves in the discussion, with results which may be very destructive.

In the debates over Judge Robert Bork this past year, and in the flurry of charges and countercharges with respect to the so-called Williamsburg Charter on religious liberty, involved but not well examined has been the function of courts in relation to great questions of human liberty. The Bork candidacy witnessed a furious debate between the Religious Right and the Irreligious Left. The Left desired to make the Senate hearings a forum for feminist and racist agendas. Bork was to be placed on the fagots and burned alive while being denounced for his sins. This was so that the nature of his sins would be better understood and that the public would learn a great lesson about how they should think on certain social issues, that they should not think at all about other social issues (for example, abortion), and that they should seethe with anger over the wicked-ness of Ronald Reagan and all "conservatives." The Religious Right, seeing all of this, decided that it must go all out for Judge Bork. He was for the Constitution. He was a "conservative." He said that he thought that *Roe* v. *Wade* was bad law. He said that he was opposed to "judge-made law." Therefore he was obviously against all that judge-made law which had banned prayer in the public schools, opened the floodgates to pornography, given criminals "rights" to commit violence, and allowed government to ride roughshod over private endeavor. And Bork was keen on "original intent," that is, the view that courts must adhere to the intentions of the drafters of the Constitution when they come to apply the Constitution to particular cases.

Conservatism did not lose in the Bork debate. Conservatism—that *real* conservatism whose core is belief in a transcendent order (Russell A. Kirk, *The Conservative Mind*, page 18) never surfaced. The Religious Right, and all the "conservative" defenders of Bork, never got to the most basic of all the issues it might have been possible to raise, namely, the question of the ultimate nature of the right, of the ultimate source of right. The supporters of Bork seemed not to listen, or to understand, what it was their martyr-hero was saying on that subject. He said that the *people* are the source of right. The people, he further argued, give us a "right" when they write it into the Constitution or when their legislatures draft it into a statute. There are no other rights. Bork completely rejected the idea expressed by the Founding Fathers in the Declaration of Independence (which is the preamble to the Preamble to the Constitution), in which they said that God was the source of our rights, that rights given by God were, in their words, "inalienable." And lest anyone should have any doubt as to where Bork stood on some of what we have deemed our most fundamental liberties, he said that he would have voted for the State of Oregon in *Pierce* v. *Society of Sisters*, which is the case in which Oregon had passed a law requiring every child to attend public school, and he would have voted for the State of Wisconsin in its criminal prosecution of Amish parents for refusing, on absolutely clear religious grounds, to send their children to high school. Further, he uttered not one syllable attacking *Roe* v. *Wade* on prolife grounds.

These crucially important points in Bork's outlook were never the subject of debate in all of the hearings. It was, oddly enough, the proabortion liberal from Pennsylvania, Senator Arlen Specter, who came closest to the issue of the true source of our rights when he asked Bork if Bork did not believe that there were certain liberties "rooted in our traditions" which courts must respect, even though they are not spelled out in constitutional wording. But Specter did that only as a tactic for embarrassing Bork, and never did Specter go beyond that to raise the question *why* something "rooted in our traditions" can be called a "right."

Let me sum up my point. One thing wrong with the current discussions between liberals and conservatives in respect to liberties and law is that the wrong conservatives are being heard from. There is, on the one hand the conservative mind described by Russell Kirk. This conservatism, while believing in such things as limited government, judicial restraint, a society governed by virtue, and the rest, holds hard to the view that our rights are God-given. Here it radically opposes the "conservatism" of the materialist conservatives (who envision no higher law than that which makes for a healthy economy), or the spurious "conservatism" of Benthamite "conservatives" who believe that the people—and especially the legislature—are the ultimate source of right.

Wrought by courts since ancient times in England, principles of natural right, derived from the teachings of the Gospels, were considered "ultimate" law. Toward the end of medieval times we see in *Dr. Bonham's Case* the Court of King's Bench saying that "when an

Act of Parliament is against common right or reason" it will be declared void. Here was an appeal to natural right, nothing vague about it. The judges still knew that God was the ultimate ruler of society, its lawgiver, and its source of right. I do not deny that there were monstrous miscarriages of justice in medieval and later Christian times. There were indeed gross acts of raw power, just as there was deliberate judicial wrongdoing in the name of "right." But even evil deeds the judges found necessary to justify according to norms ultimately found in Scripture or Christian tradition.

The great point of my dwelling upon all of this is to say that this exalted view of law—this higher law—is being discarded today, to so great an extent as to constitute a trend, by American courts, who are substituting for it a low level of law—the law of *utility*. I can best illustrate this by discussing with you some cases presently in the courts.

Utilitarianism Triumphant

In *Lyng* v. *Northwest Indian Cemetery Protective Association,* decided by the Supreme Court in 1988, the Court had before it the following facts. The Chimney Rock area of Six Rivers National Forest for at least 200 years has been used by four Indian tribes for religious rituals that critically depend upon privacy, silence, and undisturbed natural setting and access to specific sites. These tribes regard creation as an ongoing process in which they are religiously obligated to participate. They fulfill this duty by rituals intimately related to a religious view that land is a sacred, living being, and that the specific historic land sites have spiritual properties, creating an indissoluble bond between land and worshiper. The United States Forest Service in 1982 decided to construct a six-mile paved roadway through the area for general traffic and to pursue a plan for the commercial harvesting of a significant amount of timber in this area. Indians, joined by the State of California, brought suit to stop the projects as violating their free exercise of religion. The U.S. District Court granted an injunction, and the U.S. Court of Appeals for the Ninth Circuit affirmed. The U.S. Supreme Court reversed. I will not detain you by arguing the pros and cons of the competing positions of government and Indian. What is more important is the process of reasoning applied by the five-to-three majority (Justice Kennedy did not take part in the decision) in holding for the government. That opinion, by Justice Sandra Day O'Connor, is very unsettling because of its completely utilitarian character.

The opinion acknowledged that the Indians' beliefs were sincere and stated that "the government's proposed action will have devastating effects on traditional Indian religious practices." Put the Indians out of your mind for a moment as you now consider what else the Court went on to say. Think of some government action that might similarly injure your own faith community. The Court went on to say four things:

1. Though governmental action would destroy the Indians' ability to practice their religion, such action is perfectly constitutional if it does not actually coerce them into "*violating* their beliefs." Translate to non-Indian context: if government wants to demolish any church, it is free to do so. True, a church would be private property, and here was public property. But the Court's principle ignored that difference. Though its action would make it impossible for the members to worship there, though it would destroy sacred objects, though it would obliterate a hallowed edifice, the Constitution does not bar it, since government is not forcing you, say, to take some action in violation of your beliefs to desecrate your church.

2. Since (supposedly) the Indians were not being "coerced" to violate their religion, the government was not required to show that its action was justified by a "compelling state interest," some societal necessity so great as to justify the overriding even of the first right specified in the Bill of Rights—liberty of religion. Translate to non-Indian context: government is held in court to *no* obligation in reference to *constitutional* standards; its actions are self-justifying. Here we speak of what constitutional lawyers refer to as the "standard of review." That is, when the courts must pass upon a constitutional question which someone raises, how high a hurdle is government required to cross when it seeks to infringe upon personal liberties? In its *Lyng* opinion, the hurdle is simply removed. Thus utility is recognized as supreme. There must be no hurdle placed in *its* roadway. After all, as the Court says, "whatever rights the Indians may have to the use of the area . . . those rights do not divest the government of its right to use what is, after all, *its* land" for construction of a two-lane road and commercial timber harvesting.

3. Where, then, does the faith community turn for protection? The Court supplies the following interesting answer:

> The Constitution does not, and courts cannot, offer to reconcile the various competing demands on government, many of them rooted in sincere religious belief, that inevitably arise in so diverse a society as ours. That task, to the extent that it is feasible, is for legislatures and other institutions.

Flat out, if a handful of Indians in a remote region of the nation desired to protect their shrineland from immediate desecration by bulldozers and power saws, all they had to do was to (a) prepare draft legislation, (b) set up a national lobbying effort, (c) get the Congress of the United States to enact the new law as a federal statutory provision! Translate to non-Indian context: if the state is about to deny your faith community its free exercise of religion, the Free Exercise Clause may not protect you. Instead, mount a giant national legislative effort—recognizing that the Internal Revenue Service may, because of that, wipe out your tax exemption.

4. But let us examine further what the Court had to say. It then referred to *The Federalist*, No. 10, which it says suggested "that the effects of religious factionalism are best restrained through competition among a multiplicity of religious sects." The Indians' religious claim was thus further diminished by the introduction of yet another principle of utility: keeping religion from disturbing governmental plans by restraining "religious factionalism." Although *that* utilitarian principle erases the Free Exercise Clause of the Constitution, why it was involved in the Indians' case is hard to understand. Who were the religious sects that were milling about in "competition" up in Six Rivers National Forest? There were none. Don't bother to translate to non-Indian context!

Four justices of the Supreme Court—Rehnquist, White, Steven, and Scalia—joined Justice O'Connor in this opinion. It may be that, had the traditional standard of review been applied (by which the government would have been made to offer proof of a supreme societal necessity for the roadway and the timber harvesting), the decision would rightly have gone against the Indians. But, as I have pointed out, that standard was cast aside. Since this is the most recent expression of the Court on religious liberty, it is necessarily disquieting. Five justices have said, in effect: "Utility is supreme!"

I have not dealt with the *Lyng* case in order to condemn the Supreme Court. The Court, within the last decade, has provided decisions on religious liberty both good and bad. The fact that there have been some good decisions does nothing to relieve concern for the coldly materialist principles now stated as precedent which are potentially so very dangerous for the future.

The tyranny of materialist utilitarianism in the religious area is obviously dwarfed, however, by its governance in cases involving the right to life. This is no forum in which to go over again the horrors caused by *Roe* v. *Wade,* or to review in detail the new euthanasia cases. But I must point to an irony which arises when we compare the recognition of governmental power given by the courts in, on the one hand, religious liberty cases and, on the other, right to life cases. The trend in religious liberty cases heavily stresses the importance of the governmental interest. The trend in the right to life cases stresses the opposite. *Roe* v. *Wade* and its progeny decisions hold that there is actually *no* state interest warranting significant restriction on abortion practices. Take a look now at the New Jersey Supreme Court's rulings in the *Jobes, Peter*, and *Farrell* cases just a year ago. These say that the "patient's wishes" to die must come before state interests (in protecting life and caring for it). However diminishing the recognition of privacy interests in religious liberty cases, in these right to life cases privacy is everything. "Medical choices are private," said that court, "regardless of whether a patient is able to make them personally or must rely on a surrogate. They are not to be decided by societal standards of reasonableness or normalcy."

The New Jersey cases (now finding parallels in other state court decisions) are, of course, described not as "right to life" but as "right to die" litigations. They were recently described in the *New Jersey Law Journal* (Vol. 120, No. 1, page 1) as decisions which have "broken new ground," the New Jersey Supreme Court having "again reasserted itself as the nation's leader in right-to-die litigation by boldly expanding an individual's right to refuse life-sustaining medical treatment." What better example of legal utilitarianism could we have? What more Orwellian a use of language? Poor Nancy Jobes—comatose—had *exercised* her right to refuse life-sustaining treatment!

Just after these decisions, we see the California Bar Association voting to endorse a bill which would allow a doctor to give a patient a prescription-drug dose, "at the patient's request," that would cause instant death without risking prosecution of the physician by the state.

These materialist trends in the courts, observable also in many other areas of law, should be seen from two perspectives: To what do they lead? From what have they sprung? Answering those two questions, we may be in a better position to help make ourselves a society *not* in peril.

One of the predictable results of the utilitarian decisions is to encourage a like spirit in legislatures—though I am not sure that the spirit in the Congress, at least, needs much encouragement. But there does come to mind the so-called A.B.C. Bill (S. 1885, H.R. 3660), sponsored by Senator Dodd and Representative Kildee, which aims at putting all day care (and, in fact, much child care) into the hands of government. The effects of the school-secularizing decisions of the Supreme Court are felt in Sections 19 and 20 of this bill, which deny the financial *benefits* of the legislation to all meaningfully religious child care entities. The effects of the growing statism in Supreme Court decisions are felt in the fact that the bill calls for pervasive, total governmental regulation of most child care, including all meaningfully religious child care entities. The effects of decisions which disregard traditional fundamental conceptions of life are felt in the overall materialist aspect of the bill, which is careful to make provision for sex-guidance of America's children and to legislate the setting for the moulding of a whole new breed of citizen. Please allow a distinguished attorney on child care research, Dr. Elizabeth Ruppert, to be my witness here:

> By 1977 the Committee on Child Development Research and Public Policy of the NRC was formed with support from the Foundation for Child Development with the task of developing a "significantly broader and more policy-oriented approach to research and child development than has been followed in the United States." Thus began the deliberate political effort by an elite group of social scientists to "model" the environment of the family after socioeconomic policies established in northern European countries. The final research model chosen to drive U.S. social science

research directions was that of the 'working family' policy found today in Sweden.

A series of seminars, sponsored by the Swedish embassy, were then held throughout the U.S.A., while an intensive networking operation was launched to establish, in the media and in all manner of social and religious organizations, the Swedish plan. Dr. Ruppert continues:

Having adopted the "working family" socioeconomic philosophy, the National Academy of Sciences' Committee on Child Development Research and Public Policy has crossed the line from advising government to using the committee and its interlocking government agencies and affiliated institutions as a base for political activism through the generation of a research agenda designed to change the social institutions of the home, school, work and community.

The A.B.C. Bill, placed alongside the so-called Civil Rights Restoration Act of 1988 (the "Grove City" bill), placed again alongside the now (since *Bob Jones University* v. *United States*) almost total power of government to tax activity which it deems to conflict with "federal public policy," and coupled with the continuing efforts of state bureaucracies to license religious schools—and, finally, taken in conjunction with a legal regime which ever more insistently attacks traditional Christian moral principles—completes what to some appears the specter of an inevitable future of a lightless, soulless society in which frightful insecurity is bred from a frightening security.

We will begin to see how we can get our society out of peril only if we see how it got into its present peril. Is the peril due to one or more conspiracies? Of course it is, if by conspiracy we mean the clever, intense, often concealed, often deceptive maneuverings of those who, for example, well prior to *Roe* v. *Wade,* labored to change opinion on the sanctity of unborn life and spread defamation of its potential defenders. But conspiracies are only part of the picture. The larger fact is that courts (and legislatures) do not rise much higher than the moral level of the society in which they find themselves. Courts *should*, of course. In fact, at least in our time, they do not. Judges at once learn from society and rule in accordance with what they are taught. A pagan, secularist, materialist, utilitarian society has begotten judges permeated with just those values.

Willingness to Do Combat

Thank you for having heard this lawyer. People ask lawyers to see them because they want to know what to *do* about problems. Let this lawyer now tell you what can be done about the perils to our society so well stated by all the other speakers.

We Christian lawyers will do all we can to litigate, change the law, defend religion, protect the preborn, protect the terminally ill, protect the useless people, protect the young from evil manipulation by the state.

But I know that, increasingly, when we go into court, we are working in an alien medium. *We* appeal to one set of values—values which, a bare half century ago were engraved on minds and part of an immemorial tradition. But now Their Honors may have different values, values alien to the tradition. As the courts become more and more *closed* to the higher law, the more difficult it becomes to protect fundamental rights.

But we are *still* a society in which torture and Gulags are not imposed for bearing witness. We are *still* a society in which we can carry out that *obligation* to bear witness by persuading. And our case—the thing about which we are bearing witness—*is* the case that can be shown to make for the happiest life of society and individuals. And as this conference testifies, our hope lies in the lifting *up* of the society to Christ. That is the hope on which the reopening of the courts depends.

But I must carefully qualify any impression we may have that just passively living Christian lives is the answer. Our times demand in fact that we read into that the willingness to do *combat*. If we are thus willing, then I am hopeful. My hopefulness derives, both in and out of this Pentecostal season, from Christ himself. I think of him, however, not as he struggles for the dull glints of reception he finds in the timorous religious leaders of this hour in this country. These seem to feel more comfortable entering into dialogues on the agendas of *others*, in not being controversial except on behalf of secular causes popular in the media. They are terrified, not of jail, physical violence, or exile (*these* are not at hand) but of bad media image or potential defamation by people of bad will. But I think of Christ as the disciples thought of him in Acts 4. How refreshing it is to read

> And Annas the high priest, and Caiaphas, and John, and Alexander, and as many as were of the kindred of the high priest, were gathered together at Jerusalem. And when they had set them in the midst, they asked, By what power, or by what name, have ye done this? Then Peter, filled with the Holy Ghost, said unto them, Ye rulers of the people, and elders of Israel, if we this day be examined of the good deed done to the impotent man, by what means he is made whole; be it known unto you all, and to all the people of Israel, that by the name of Jesus Christ of Nazareth, whom ye crucified, whom God raised from the dead, even by him doth this man stand here before you whole. This is the stone which was set at nought of you builders, which is become the head of the corner. Neither is there salvation in any other: for there is none other name under heaven given among men, whereby we must be saved. Now when they saw the boldness of Peter and John, and perceived that they were unlearned and ignorant men, they marvelled; and they took knowledge of them, that they had been with Jesus.

That says it all.

TWO

How the Press Treats and Mistreats Religious News

Marvin Olasky

I HAVE BEEN FEELING GUILTY ABOUT SPEAKING to you this afternoon. The fact that I am here right now, and the fact that you are here, indicates that we are not next door listening to J. I. Packer. When I saw the schedule, I wondered: Should I be here, should anyone be here, why would anyone *want* to be here, learning about journalism, when we could be learning about theology?

It so happened that over at Fisher Hall my suite-mate has been J.I. Packer himself. I was sharing a bathroom with him, trying to keep it very clean. About 45 minutes ago, as I was brushing my teeth, which is a good thing to do before giving a speech, there was Dr. Packer. I told him about my trepidation. He said in a very kind way, "Nonsense. There is nothing more crucial in America than for Christians to reclaim the media. Think of what it could mean if this were accomplished in this generation."

So that guilt of mine has been now laid to rest by Dr. Packer himself. That is why we are all here. We are not just here to do media bashing. That is easy to do. It is worthwhile in some ways. There are certainly a lot of reasons to bash the media. But we are not just here to complain. We are here to reclaim the media. We are not placing the worldly above the spiritual. We are here to claim all things for Christ.

Charles Colson last night mentioned Tom Brokaw's bias. Mr. Colson noted that Brokaw "is dispassionate in his reporting—but that is the point. Today's barbarians are civilized." That is a very nice expression, and it is certainly true about today's media leaders. It is incredible what network journalists can do technologically—not only the types of information they have available to them, but also their coolness under fire. I recently saw the movie, *Broadcast News*. A few of you have seen it. One reporter gets his big chance as an anchorman on the weekend news. He has a case of the terminal sweats, just incredible perspiration, and that is the end of his anchoring career. Even if Tom Brokaw were here yesterday in the heat, you would not expect to see him sweating. He seems totally dispassionate, totally controlled, totally above all the usual facts of human nature—and he wants to appear that way. That is the key to being a successful anchor. An anchorman is trained to appear totally unruffled under any circumstances, totally in control, totally above the news.

This is the culmination of what has been developing in American journalism for many decades now: newspeople are to share somewhat in the attributes of a god, twentieth-century variety. They are totally above. They are looking down on us. They have no ideology as such. They have no worldview. They are perhaps not exactly omnipotent, but at least omniscient, all-seeing, and they have the technology to back up that claim. If you go and talk with a network leading man and say, "Surely you have a worldview of some kind, and surely it must affect the way you report the news," he will say, publicly at least, "No. Not at all. I am a professional. I don't get involved in this, and no matter how far you prod me, I will stick to my story."

There is a Texas story about an old Dallas lawyer who came back home one night and lied to his wife about where he had been. He said that he had been at the house of a dear sick lady in the neighborhood, just trying to be kind to her. His wife said, "Well, that could not be, because I called her just half an hour ago, and you hadn't been there." And he, with great Texas peace of mind, drew himself up and said, "That may be true, but nevertheless, I am sticking to my story." That is the way it is with a number of leading media people. No matter how much you point out instances of bias, leading journalists stick to the story of objectivity. Some reporters themselves believe in the myth, others do not.

Let's look at those who see proclamation of the myth as useful self-defense. Say you are a pro-abortion reporter (according to surveys, 90 percent of elite journalists are very definitely pro-abortion). How does a journalist try to help the abortion side, while still proclaiming his neutrality?

One trick of the trade is what I refer to as the ABABCCC pattern. Namely, you take a spokesman for the pro-abortion point of view (position A), and you quote that person. Then in the next paragraph you quote a person from the prolife point of view (position B). Then maybe you do it again—ABAB—so that you are quoting people from both sides. Often you try to find the smartest person you can for the pro-abortion point of view, and the most tongue-tied person you can from the pro-life point of view, and then quote them. Nevertheless, you do have ABAB. But then you bring in C, and another C, and another C; and the C is someone who is an "expert" on the question, someone who has, perhaps, a PhD after his name. The expert, C, will always be a person from the pro-abortion point of view. He will be that person who is supposed to answer the questions, "What is really going on? Who is telling the truth in this argument?" The expert will be there to say that the pro-abortion person is right and the anti-abortion person is dumb. You see this over and over and over again. Now it may be that there are more people with PhDs after their name who are pro-abortion than prolife. I am not sure about that, but it may be. Nevertheless, there are plenty of experts on the prolife side. But you very rarely see them quoted as experts. That is just one example of the technique that journalists use to make a biased story appear neutral and objective.

We had our graduation at the University of Texas a week ago, and our town's newspaper ran a feature story about a woman who had had an unhappy childhood, dropped out of high school, and was a truck driver for a couple of years. She had been an alcoholic. Now her life had turned around. She was graduating from the University of Texas, and it was a very happy day. As Christians we can see God's providence in the way her life has changed. But this is the way it was reported in the newspaper: "It was luck that she found a textbook on psychology one day at the grocery store, and reading it inspired her to resume an education that had been angrily cast aside years before. It was luck that she decided to get educated while she was still eligible for financial aid because her mother is a World War II veteran in

Canada. It was luck that, when she was working for a delivery service in Austin, while attending Austin Community College, she was sent to the University of Texas one day, passed the admissions office, and picked up an application." Now this was a very serious *religious* view, essentially, that was being put forth by the reporter, an explanation of why things happen as they do. Things happen because of chance, the newspaper suggested. I call this "Wheel of Fortune" journalism.

Wheel of Fortune is the most popular game show on television. It is often put on right opposite the local news or the evening network news. It always gets high ratings. The newspeople complain about that like crazy. Pat Sajak, the emcee of *Wheel of Fortune* (which is also known for Vannah White, "the letter turner"), was asked, "Do you have any advice for Tom Brokaw?" He said, "Tom, get a wheel." But in many ways that is what we have. This story I just told you about the University of Texas graduate is an example. In many ways, what we see on the local news is "Wheel of Fortune" reporting: things just happen. Spin the wheel, and sometimes things turn out well. Sometimes, people are lucky, but sometimes unlucky. That is the way things go. There is no sense of God's sovereignty, no sense of providence. Chance is running our lives.

That, of course, is one of the oldest religions in the world—the belief that chance is behind everything. It is a religious view that, of course, is not expressed as religious. It is a religious point of view that is presented every day on the nightly news and in newspapers.

I will give you another example, an Illinois story from Winetka, not far from here. It happened about a week and a half ago. A woman named Laurie Dann went into a school and started shooting. A school child was killed and others were wounded. What is the cause of this? Why did it happen? You see, every newspaper reporter is taught in journalism school or on his first day on the job to ask six questions: who, what, when, where, how, and why. The idea is that if you are going to write a complete news story, you are supposed to answer all six of those questions.

I submit to you that "why" is a worldview question. Why do things happen? What is the cause of them? "Why" takes us to questions about the nature of man and the nature of God. Reporters covering Laurie Dann asked why. Here is the explanation an AP story gave: "She saw herself as a victim. She sought revenge against those who had diminished her sense of self-worth." We were also given some psychobabble: she may have suffered from a borderline personality disorder or paranoid psychosis. And we were told that she had not received help from various social agencies. All of this may be very true. But is that *the* reason why? We as Christians know that there is such a thing as sin. It is present in the world. It is real. It affects the way we act. In fact, there is a creature called Satan who tries to take advantage of our sinful tendencies. So it is not enough to talk about victimhood or the failures of various agencies, as if more psychologists or social workers would prevent such problems. Stories that minimize individual responsibility and see problems arising primarily from societal failures are stories that proclaim a particular view. They are not objective. They are not neutral.

Stories that address the why by stressing either chance or institutional failures show an anti-Christian bias. They are anti-Christian not because they are prejudiced on some of the hot issues of the 1980's—the battles between Christians and evolutionists in schools, questions of prayer, questions of the role of Christians in politics, or whatever. On those you see explicit bias coming through. But that bias is easy to point to. I get more interested in examples of the more subtle bias, the way that, story after story, there is a tendency to minimize personal responsibility for action. There is always a tendency in these stories to see a social cause for problems— a cause external to man. The cause is located in institutional breakdown that leads people to act in bad ways. On this view, sin does not exist. Problems exist, but the answer or solution we are given for the most part is a governmental program. For example, if we have problems in families, we need a governmental program. We have seen a rash of this over the past couple of months in the campaign to have a national system of child care. News stories about this issue are religious stories also. They are based on a view of man in which personal responsibility questions of sin are minimized. Problems occur because of corrupt institutions or other factors external to man. The way to live happily ever after is to set up the right social institutions. Without the right social institutions, chance and anarchy rule. With the right institutions, wise planners rule. That is a religious view with its own eschatology.

What happens when there are stories with very clear religious components? I have done research on the newspaper coverage of a hero of mine, a fellow named Whitaker Chambers. He was a

Communist party member and spy during the 1930s. Then he was born again. He became a spokesman for Christianity and against Communism and wrote a very powerful book called *Witness*. When he was in the public spotlight because of his testimony, reporters asked him why he had given up his powerful job on *Time* magazine. He had been well-paid. The reporters could not understand why he gave it all up to become a witness, unless he was crazy. Chambers said that somebody had to be out there criticizing the great alternative faith of mankind, "the Communist vision of man without God . . . man's mind displacing God as the creative intelligence of the world."

Chambers testified that he had been consumed by that sinful vision until God had changed his heart through free grace. Sin and grace: Chambers's story of conversion from Communism to Christianity was impossible to understand unless those concepts were taken seriously. But the journalists just could not consider sin and grace as facts of human life. They constantly implied that Chambers had to be wacko. The reporters were unable to even begin to report Chambers's story intelligently, not because they were deliberately out to get him, although many of them were, but because they did not understand. This was forty years ago, when there was more evidence of Christian understanding in some parts of society than there is now.

What happens when prayer is a large part of the story? Let me give you a recent example: coverage of the overthrow of Ferdinand Marcos in the Philippines. You probably read accounts of the numbers of guns and tanks on each side—but did you read anything in major newspapers about the power of prayer? I later read a story in a Christian magazine by one missionary who was there. He wrote, "What accounted for the fact that the military forces did not overrun the crowds? They had sufficient tear gas and water cannons to disperse the people. But they didn't use them. What kept hundreds of thousands of people from becoming a wild uncontrolled mob? What held their emotions in check? What enabled the crowds to show kindness and offer food and drink to their enemies in the government forces?" According to the account by the missionary, millions of Filipinos were praying. Prayer was efficacious in that situation. But none of the reporters there could take seriously the belief that God might actually answer prayers, not by making us feel better, but by transforming earthly situations (of course, not always in the way we expect). We do not know what will happen in the Philippines down the road. But as Christians we do know that God helps us and disciplines us because of the amazing love that he has for us. Reporters just could not deal with that at all. They did not report the praying as they did the guns and tanks. The result was not neutral reporting. It was radically incomplete reporting. It was reporting that looked at the material factors involved but completely omitted—spiked—the spiritual.

In short the real difficulty that we face in claiming American journalism for Christ is not that Christian activities do not get the coverage they often deserve. The difficulty is not that some raunchy activities may get more coverage than they deserve. The problem is that journalists are proclaiming a different religion, an anti-Christian religion. It is a mixture of two kinds of very old religions: one, the Wheel of Fortune religion, where everything just happens by chance, and the other, a type of materialistic determinism, holding that there is no such thing as real individual responsibility, no such thing as sin. In this view, evil does not come from inside, it comes from outside. Journalists typically proclaim that man is good by nature and is just corrupted by institutions. If only we can find the magic bullet, the key to transform particular institutions, then we will live happily ever after. For some journalists, the real problem is private property. That is what creates the problem. So if we got rid of capitalism, we would all live happily ever after. For others there are other reasons. But there is always the search for something external to man, rather than something internal.

Reclaiming the Media

Enough about the problem. I now want to suggest a way to begin solving it. But to see the future, we need to understand the past. What happened to Christian journalism? After all, during its first couple of centuries American journalism *was* Christian journalism. That is something that history books now totally ignore. But all you have to do is look at some of those old newspapers. Read the way they reported things. You will see that they tried to have complete coverage, complete in the sense of looking at both the spiritual and the material.

Before the Civil War, newspapers and magazines with explicitly

Christian emphases covered everything from neighborhood disputes to foreign affairs. They did not restrict themselves to church activities. For example, the Boston *Recorder* included news of everyday accidents, crimes, political campaigns, and so on. It soon had the second largest circulation in New England.

Here is an example of one of the exciting stories it ran: An eyewitness account in 1822 of an earthquake in Syria. There were descriptions of "men and women clinging to the ruined walls of their houses, holding their children in their trembling arms; mangled bodies lying under my feet, and piercing cries of half buried people assailing my ears." Others were "falling on their knees and imploring the mercy of God; and, shortly after, crowding the places of worship, eager to learn what they must do to be saved." A *Recorder* editorial then described other great earthquakes and asked, "Should not the awful demonstrations of divine power cause us to fear him who can so suddenly sweep away a whole city into destruction? Should not sinners tremble to think how awful it is to have such a God for an enemy? Should they not immediately seek reconciliation to him through the blood of the Lamb?"

Christian newspapers up to the mid-19th century attempted to provide a biblical worldview on all aspects of life. One Ohio newspaper declared in 1858 that the Christian newspaper should be a provider of not "merely religious intelligence, but a *news* paper, complete in every department of general news, yet upon a religious, instead of a political or literary basis." Another, the *Northwestern Christian Advocate*, proclaimed in 1860, "Let theology, law, medicine, politics, literature, art, science, commerce, trade, architecture, agriculture—in fine, all questions which concern and secure the welfare of a people—be freely discussed and treated, and this, too, for God, for Jesus Christ, and for the advancement of the redeemer's kingdom among men."

Overall, many early Christian journalists showed an awareness of how the Bible uses bad news to show us the wages of sin and to prepare us for understanding the necessity of the good news. The journalists knew that general statements about man's corruption were far less gripping than coverage with specific detail of the results of sin and misery. The New York *Times*, for example, had a great exposé of abortion, headlined "The Evil of the Age."

The story began on a solemn note: "Thousands of human beings are murdered before they have seen the light of this world." There was a description of the back of one abortionist's office: "Human flesh, supposed to have been the remains of infants, was found in barrels of lime and acids, undergoing decomposition." The *Times* listed leading abortionists by name and noted their political connections. One *Times* anti-abortion editorial concluded, "It is useless to talk of such matters with bated breath, or to seek to cover such terrible realities with the veil of a false delicacy. . . . From a lethargy like this it is time to rouse ourselves. The evil that is tolerated is aggressive; if we want the good to exist at all, it must be aggressive too." The *Times* was instrumental in obtaining tough anti-abortion laws in New York at that time.

But aggressive journalism by Christians disappeared. Many Christian publications began to prefer "happy talk" journalism. They ran stories about individuals who seemed overwhelmingly decent, cooperative, responsible, and benevolent. Such coverage hardly left the impression that man is a fallen creature desperately in need of Christ. The publications also became boring. Without coverage of evil they were left without real drama.

Underlying all this was a theological trend among Christians. As historian George Marsden has noted, the 1860-1900 period brought with it "a transition from a basically 'Calvinistic' tradition, which saw politics as a significant means to advance the kingdom, to a 'pietistic' view of political action as no more than a means to restrain evil." Social concerns became suspect among revivalist evangelicals. Many Christians began to believe that the general culture inevitably would become worse and worse. They thought that little could be done to stay the downward drift. Christian publications should cover church news, they thought, and ignore the rest of the world.

I do not want to minimize the immense social and theological changes of the late nineteenth century. Powerful intellectual trends undercut orthodox belief. Darwinism. Marxism. Biblical "higher criticism." A general emphasis on "science" as mankind's savior. But in biblical times when God's people saw the Assyrians or the Babylonians defeating Israel, they did not explain the defeat by saying the enemy was irresistible. The Bible said that God was chastising the believers for turning away from true faith, and for not converting faith into action. Read Jeremiah 16.

The failure of commitment, rather than the power of the opposition, is the lesson I take away from the nineteenth century experience. It was not cheap to start up those early Christian newspapers, but many early Christians were committed. They saw purchase of printing presses and offices every bit as important as pulpit activity. That confidence in reaching out diminished throughout the nineteenth century. Defeatist thinking about the tendencies of American society took over. The result was that God was expelled from the front page. By the early twentieth century, Christians often were voiceless, except in publications that largely preached to the choir.

In other words, if we want to see why anti-Christians now dominate the press we have to know that Christians gave up on it. Now, though, God is giving us a second chance. Just look at the new technology. Luther called printing "God's highest and extremest act of grace, whereby the business of the gospel is driven forward." John Foxe, the Puritan journalist, wrote of "the excellent arte of printing most happily of late found out . . . to the singular benefite of Christe's church." We might say the same thing about new opportunities opening up to Christians now through desktop publishing, computerization in newspaper, magazine, and newsletter publishing, and new broadcasting technology, such as cable and satellite.

Christians now have the opportunity to put out newsletters, weekly newspapers, and eventually daily newspapers, that can really challenge the monopoly on the news that the secular orthodoxy tends to have. It is not expensive anymore to start up a publication through what is called desktop publishing, using computers and the graphics that can be developed in that way. Invest $5,000 buying a computer and a laser printer, and you are in business.

The question is, how will you attract readers? Providentially, the Bible—Carl Henry once called it "God's newspaper"—provides us a model. I would like us here to look particularly at its vividness of description. For example, the five books of Moses culminate in the blessing for obedience and curses of disobedience found in chapter 28 of Deuteronomy. Israelites are told that unfaithfulness will lead to terrible war and starvation in which "you will eat the flesh of the womb, the flesh of the sons and daughters the Lord your God has given you . . . The most gentle and sensitive woman among you—so sensitive and gentle that she would not venture to touch the ground with the sole of her foot—will begrudge the husband she loves and her own son or daughter the afterbirth from her womb and the children she bears. For she intends to eat them secretly."

The ethical slide downhill was speedy during the period described in the Book of Judges. When God wanted to show us the effect of the Israelites ignoring him—"There was no king in Israel"—his inspired author wrote of a man murdering his 70 brothers and half-brothers. The Book of Judges tells of a woman being gang raped and killed, with her husband cutting her into twelve pieces and then sending the body parts throughout Israel. Specific detail was not left out: Jael's assassination of Sisera was described in five graphic ways. When Ehud plunged his sword into the belly of the king of Moab, pungent description follows: "Even the handle sank in after the blade, which came out his back. Ehud did not pull the sword out, and the fat closed in over it."

By the time of Ahab and his son Joram, some of the curses for disobedience already were being realized. One woman told the king, "This woman said to me, 'Give up your son so we may eat him today, and tomorrow we'll eat my son.' So we cooked my son and ate him. The next day I said to her, 'Give up your son so we may eat him,' but she had hidden him." Ezekiel promoted similar disgust at what God's covenant people had become. He wrote of how Judah "lusted after her lovers, whose genitals were like those of donkeys and whose emissions was like that of horses. So you longed for the lewdness of your youth, when in Egypt your bosom was caressed and your young breasts fondled."

Specific detail! Vivid depiction of the results of sin! Jeremiah explained God's journalistic methods when he wrote: "This is what the Lord Almighty, the God of Israel, says: Listen! I am going to bring a disaster on this place that will make the ears of everyone who hears of it tingle." Romans, Revelation, and other books of the New Testament have graphic descriptions also. Just ask yourself the question: How can ears tingle if descriptions are mellow?

We do not have to look far, then, for a way to get readers to pay attention to Christian writing. We should follow the example of God and his inspired writers, and make proper use of what I would call *biblical sensationalism*. A Christian reporter following the biblical examples can see that he should try to provide as complete an account as he can—spiritual and material, joy and misery. If a Christian wants to report only the elevating and not the depressing, he forgets that in

Christianity there is no repentance without an awareness of sin, no triumph without suffering, no resurrection without the cross.

Christian journalism should not shrink from showing man as sinner, fully responsible before God who requires obedience. Christian journalism should make ears tingle at the news of punishment for breaking God's law. It should educate readers or viewers against the belief that sin is without consequences. It should be the two-by-four that is often necessary to gain our attention. For example, on abortion, Christian publications should not just run editorials against abortion, but should go undercover into abortion businesses and show in detail exactly what abortionists do to make a living. I would like to see more names, home addresses, and telephone numbers of abortionists prominently displayed, preferably on billboards. I could explain more about the uses of this approach in other specific areas, but I think you get the idea: Follow the biblical pattern of throwing a spotlight on the workings of evil.

I have been speaking for 45 minutes, and I'd like to give some other specific prescriptions, but it is important to allow time for questions. Those of you interested in the subject might look at my books *Prodigal Press* or *The Press and Abortion*. For now, for Christians called to work in journalism, let me emphasize: The technology is here. The methodology is here. I have confidence that, if we follow Biblical principles, God's blessings will be here. As Dr. Packer said, think about what it could mean if Christians reclaimed the media. Doing that will be hard work. Journalism is a rough business. A tough business. But for what are we here on earth, except to work hard to glorify God and, through Christ's sacrifice for us, to enjoy him forever?

THREE

Government, Individualism, and Mediating Communities

Francis Canavan

WE HAVE IN THIS COUNTRY a pluralistic society, and one which is becoming more pluralistic all the time, not only in a growing diversity of religious belief but, far more important, a growing division in moral belief and practice. This pluralistic society is organized and governed under a constitutional liberal democracy. There are three terms in that phrase: democratic, liberal, and constitutional. Of these three terms, the most important is constitutional.

What is constitutionalism? It is not by definition liberalism or democracy. You could have, and historically we have had, constitutional governments which were not democratic and not necessarily liberal. What constitutionalism means is simply limited government. If government is limited in its power and in its functions, it is a constitutional government. That does not necessarily imply a written constitution. As Americans, we think so. But Great Britain has not had a single document that you can point to and say, that is the British constitution. Constitutionalism simply means the idea of limited government and, therefore, a society which is free precisely because the powers of government are limited.

Now the limits on government are three: legal, political, and social. First, the legal limits on government. Here is a passage from a series of lectures given at Cornell University forty years ago by Professor Charles McIlwain of Harvard, who was the leading authority on the history of political thought in his day. At that time, McIlwain said, "In all its successive phases, constitutionalism has had one essential quality: it is a legal limitation on government; it is the antithesis of arbitrary rule; its opposite is despotic government, the government of will instead of law. . . . but the most ancient, the most persistent, and the most lasting of the essentials of true constitutionalism still remains what it has been almost from the beginning: the limitation of government by law." In this country, we tend to think of that as the only limitation on government.

But there are others. For example, there is the political limitation. Government is limited when it needs to get the consent of the people to what it does. The people need not be the entire population. Certainly in eighteenth-century Britain the politically effective people were not the entire population or even a very large part of it. But you did have an elected House of Commons. This connotes the ability of the people legally and peacefully to change the personnel of government. As McIlwain pointed out, government in the Middle Ages was considered to be limited government, but unfortunately, there was no *legal* way to change it. The barons had to get together and put their lances on King John's chest and say, "Sign here." And then, under compulsion, he signed Magna Carta.

The political limitation on government means that the people through the process of election can change the personnel of government. When you extend the notion of the people to include the entire adult population, then you have democracy and, combined with legal limits on the powers of government, it is a constitutional democracy.

The third limit on the power of government is a social one. It consists in the existence of institutions which government did not create, but whose rights and influence it must respect. There are many things that a government in Washington will not try to do if big business, big agriculture, and big labor, or any two of them, seriously object to it. That is very important, and that is the burden of what I want to say today. These are the so-called mediating or intermediary institutions which stand as a check upon the power of government and, therefore, as a guarantee of the freedom of the people. They thus limit the power of government over individuals.

What are the mediating institutions? There are many definitions of them. Let me read you one from a recent book called *Cultural Conservatism*. "Mediating institutions stand between the individual citizen and government and, thereby, prevent the reduction of society to lone individuals facing an immensely powerful, all-pervasive state apparatus." The most important mediating institution is the family. Among the others are churches, professional associations, labor unions, businesses, service organizations, and a free press.

Now modern liberal constitutional thought, which had its origins in the seventeenth-century in the writings of men like Thomas Hobbes and John Larkin, has tended from its beginning to limit the powers of government by guaranteeing the rights of individuals. I read somewhere recently, and I think it is true, that liberalism had two great objectives; it accomplished them, and they were great accomplishments. One of them was to put an end to religious strife in Europe by bringing in a regime of religious toleration. The other was to curb the power of kings, who everywhere on the continent, and almost in England, had succeeded in making themselves absolute monarchs. Both of these were good things to do. But it is worth remembering that what people do, and their motives for doing it, and the theory by which they explain this to themselves and others, are not one and the same thing. Liberalism developed an ideology to justify and explain what it was trying to do. Since the ideology was flawed and defective, certain consequences have followed from that.

What was the ideology? Well, in fashioning it, you hypothesized a state of nature, the natural condition that human beings were in, a situation in which there was no civil society under government and law. The state of nature was populated by individuals, each of whom was an independent entity, sovereign over himself and beholden, if at all, only to a law of nature which was given by God. But this degenerated, naturally, into a state of anarchy because everyone was a judge in his own cause whenever there was a dispute over conflicting interpretations of rights. Resorts to force inevitably happened.

So then you formed a social contract. All these independent individuals came together and said, "We are killing one another. Let us contract to surrender enough of our liberty to set up a government that can settle disputes and protect our rights because it will have the force to make its decisions obeyed." That becomes the foundation of society. Its only purpose is to protect the rights of individuals. For the rest, they are on their own.

That view was a break with the medieval conception of constitu-tionalism, which limited the power of the king by his subjection to age-old law. Bracton, the English legal authority in the thirteenth century, had said, "The king is under no man, but under God and the law." In the Middle Ages, the law was customary law. No one made it. It had always been there since the mind of man runneth not to the contrary, and it was superior to king and people alike. The other check on the power of kings in the Middle Ages was the rights and powers of the church, the nobility, the universities, the chartered towns, and the holders of property. These were the intermediary institutions whose rights the king had to respect, and that remained true even under the absolute monarchy of France, right up to the French Revolution.

But from the late Middle Ages on, political theory, the way in which people conceptualized the problem of politics, focused more and more on drawing the line between the state and the individual. The German authority, Otto Gierke, says this in a book which was translated into English under the title, *Political Theories of the Middle Ages*: "The Sovereign State and the Sovereign Individual contended over the delimitation of the provinces assigned to them by Natural Law, and in the course of that struggle all intermediate groups were first degraded into the position of the more or less arbitrarily fashioned creatures of mere Positive Law and, in the end, were obliterated." Which is to say that as people thought about politics, what it was, what it was supposed to accomplish, they conceptualized it in terms of the state versus the individual. The necessary power of the state and the necessary rights of the individual were the two and only two poles of political thought. That has heavily influenced our constitutional thought from the beginning of modern times, but particularly, I would say, since the Second World War.

Recent constitutional law in the United States has limited government by insisting more and more upon individual rights. Still more recently, so has civil rights legislation enacted by Congress or by the several state legislatures. This undoubtedly limits what government may do to individuals, but by the same token, and necessarily, it increases what government may do *for* individuals and *to* institutions. That, I think, is something that deserves our attention, because government today is obliged to be, at one and the same time, individualistic and statist. Government is individualistic when it serves an expanding array of individual rights. But insofar as it uses the power of the state to impose these rights upon institutions, government is statist, and the fingers of the bureaucracy reach more and more into all of the institutions of society.

Our constitutionalism today is a blend of libertarianism and egalitarianism. It emancipates the individual from all norms that he himself has not consented to. No one can tell me what to think, or to say, or to do, up to the point where I start impinging upon the equal rights of other people. But there is no public norm that can be imposed upon me, unless it is justified in the name of the equal liberty of everyone to follow his own beliefs and his own moral norms. The imposition of this particular individualistic conception of liberty upon the institutions of society is what I mean by egalitarianism. It is a particular conception of equality.

The Weakening of Intermediary Institutions

Now I would like to read you a passage which comes to the heart of what I want to say. I found this in an article by Stanley Hauerwas, a Methodist theologian, now teaching in the divinity school at Duke University. In this article, which he wrote some six years ago, he said, "The very means that are used to insure that the democratic state be a limited state—namely, the rights of the individual—turn out to be no less destructive for intermediate institutions than the monistic state of Marxism. For it is the strategy of liberalism to ensure the existence of the autonomy of cultural and economic life by insuring the freedom of the individual. Ironically, that strategy results in the undermining of intermediate institutions, because they are now understood only as those arbitrary institutions sustained by the private desires of individuals."

What does he mean by that? In his lectures at this conference, Charles Colson said there are three given, objective, God-willed institutions: the family, the state, and the church. Two of these, the family and the state, are natural, the church is supernatural. But they are not created and they are not sustained by the private desires of individuals. Hauerwas said in his article that whatever else the family is, it is not simply a voluntary institution.

Obviously, in one sense, it is voluntary. No one has to get married. If you do marry, you do not have to marry this one rather than that one. John marries Mary because John and Mary consent to marry one another. If you look at it closely, that is what a marriage ceremony is. It is the open declaration of consent to this particular union, and without it, John and Mary are not married. But notice that what they consent to is simply marrying one another. They do not determine what marriage is. They can enter it or not, with this person or another person. But they cannot determine to marry for a year and a day, or for five days a week with weekends off, or to have a situation in which three persons live happily ever after, or marry a person of the same sex. The nature of marriage does not depend on their consent at all. As with the other basic institutions of society, marriage does not depend upon our individual private consent.

Hauerwas's point, and the one that I want to convey this afternoon, is that by our insistence on seeing the only check upon the power of the state as being the private rights of individuals, we are seriously undermining these intermediate institutions.

Recent Instances

Let me give you a few instances of this out of many that one could recite. One is the Grove City case. Grove City College is a small, private, liberal arts college in Pennsylvania. You are probably all familiar with Hillsdale College in Michigan. Both of them were brought to court by the government, but the Supreme Court decided it would take the Grove City case and, in deciding it, was really deciding for both colleges. These are both colleges that had steadfastly refused to accept any federal funds, one reason being that Title IX of the Education Act of 1972 requires a school, if it receives federal funds, to comply with federal regulations issued under the Education Act banning various forms of discrimination.

The bureaucratic agency of the government that was concerned with administering these regulations wrote to Grove City College and told its administrators that they were obliged to fill out forms saying that they had complied with the requirements of this act. One of the complaints against them was that they had practiced sex discrimination by insisting that young men and young women play on separate teams in athletic sports. Grove City said it did not have to comply, because it had not received federal money. The bureaucrats said that it had received federal funds because it had students who had student loans and grants, and that put federal money into the college, and therefore it was obliged by the act.

The case went to court, and the Supreme Court decided, in a Solomonic decision, to split the baby in two. That is to say, the Court decided that Grove City College was indeed obliged by the act to the extent that the federal funds coming into the school affected its programs. But since the funds were in the form of student aid, they would affect only the admissions office and the financial aid office, nothing else in the school

For four years after that decision various civil rights groups labored to get Congress to pass a law clarifying what they meant in the 1972 act. This finally went through Congress in the spring of this year, in the Civil Rights Restoration Act of 1988. This act says that if you are running a private institution (it need not be a school; it could be a hospital or an orphanage) and federal money is coming to it in any way, you are obliged to comply with all the regulations issued under the various civil rights laws passed by Congress.

Once a law is passed, it gets out of the hands of Congress and is turned over to the administrative agencies, the bureaucracy, which then spell out its meaning by issuing guidelines or regulations. If you want to contest them, you have to go to court and persuade the court that the federal regulations are not what Congress intended. So there is a transfer of power from the legislative branch of the government, the Congress, to the executive, or administrative branch, and ultimately, to the judicial branch.

There was no great public reaction against the Civil Rights Restoration Act. President Reagan vetoed the act and it went back to Congress. I have read that at this point evangelical groups woke up and began to deluge Congress with protests urging Congress not to override the president's veto. But as *Time* magazine remarked, the Republicans did not dare to vote against anything called a civil rights act in an election year and, of course, the Democrats wanted it from the beginning, because among their important constituent groups are precisely the people who wanted this kind of law. Congress passed the act over the president's veto, and the result is a further extension of federal power into private institutions in this country.

An even more extreme example is the Georgetown University case, which is simply one example, the most extreme, of the gay rights laws that have been passed in many cities in this country. For example, a year or two ago the City of New York told all church-related agencies performing services for the city under contract—like running orphanages and foster care—that they would have to agree to nondiscrimination in the employment of homosexuals. The Catholic Church in New York was in an interim, in which the previous archbishop had died and the new one had not been appointed; so it did nothing. But the Salvation Army, to its credit, stood up and just said no, and the Jewish organization, Agudath Israel, said no, and finally, when Cardinal John O'Connor came in as archbishop of the Catholic archdiocese, he said no. These institutions went to court and got a declaration from the court that the mayor had acted beyond his power in issuing this executive order. He then got it through as an ordinance of the city council, but with an exception for the religious groups. That is the kind of thing you are up against all the time.

Let us go back to the Georgetown University case. The District of Columbia passed an antidiscrimination ordinance making it unlawful for an educational institution to deny access to any of its facilities and services to persons otherwise qualified—namely, students—for reasons based upon the race, color, religion, national origin, sex, age, marital status, personal appearance, sexual orientation, family responsibilities, political affiliations, source of income, or physical handicap of any individual. (If you can think of any other possible ground of discrimination, please write to the District of Columbia government, and I am sure they will put it into the law.)

Now Georgetown had a homosexual students organization on campus. In a way, it is really hard to prevent that. Any group of students can get together and meet with one another and talk with one another and call themselves whatever they want. I do not see any effective way of stopping them from doing that. What you can do is deny them official recognition as a student organization and any funds from the student government. That is what Georgetown did. So the homosexual students went to court under the District of Columbia ordinance. The university won in the trial court. That decision, however, was appealed to the Court of Appeals of the

District of Columbia, the highest municipal court in the district, and it decided against Georgetown.

Georgetown then decided not to fight the case up to the Supreme Court. I had hoped that they would, on the premise that if you go to the Supreme Court, even if you lose, at least you can tell your alumni that you carried the fight right to the end and it is perfectly clear that the decision was forced upon you. Georgetown did not do that. I have a letter that was sent out by the president of Georgetown in which he explains why he did not do it.

One reason, I must admit, from a lawyer's point of view carries a certain amount of weight, and it is this. Justice Scalia is a graduate of Georgetown, and he therefore would disqualify himself from sitting on the decision of this case. This left Georgetown facing the very strong possibility of a split 4-4 decision in the Supreme Court, which would uphold the decision of the lower court. It may be that Georgetown acted wisely in not taking the case to the Supreme Court.

Be that as it may, let me read just one line from the letter of the president. He said that "Despite the scattering of opinions in the Court of Appeals of the District of Columbia, the holding of the court is clear. The District of Columbia has a compelling interest in eradicating discrimination against homosexuals that overrides the First Amendment protection of Georgetown's religious objections to subsidizing homosexual organizations." The rights of individual homosexuals override the right of a religious institution not to tolerate upon its campus organizations in direct, open conflict with its moral teaching. That is one example of why I think that there can be and often is a conflict between the rights of individuals and the rights of intermediary institutions.

Finally, I read an article not long ago on the effect of United States Supreme Court decisions on marriage and the family. I will give you a couple of samples. In 1965 the Court decided the case of *Griswold* v. *Connecticut*. It held unconstitutional a law of the State of Connecticut making use of contraceptives illegal. It was obviously an unenforceable law, and the Supreme Court had twice turned down cases contesting it, on the ground that nobody had ever been prosecuted under it and, therefore, no one was suffering. But in 1964 the justices of the Court were persuaded to take the Griswold case, and they decided in favor of the plaintiffs against the State of Connecticut because they discovered in the Constitution a right of privacy, nowhere mentioned in the Constitution in so many words, but which would include the privacy of the marital relation against intrusion by the state. Subsequent decisions of the Court have extended this right of privacy to bar state interference with the sale and dissemination of contraceptives to unmarried persons. Privacy has also been interpreted to include the right to abortion.

In 1972, in the case of *Loving* v. *Virginia*, the Court found that an interracial couple, a black-white marriage, who were prosecuted in Virginia for violating a Virginia state law against interracial marriage, had a right to marry which the State of Virginia was violating. The Court said that the Constitution guarantees a fundamental right to marry. I think we would all agree that there is such a thing as a natural right of people to marry, and that it is a basic right. But before we stand up and cheer for that, let us look at some of the consequences that the Supreme Court has drawn from it. For example, they have extended the right to marry and, therefore, an immunity from state regulation of access to that right, to include divorce and a right to remarry after divorce, because all of these are aspects of fundamental human right. I think it was in 1979 that a statute of the State of Wisconsin was contested before the Court. Wisconsin had provided by law that if you were divorced and were under court order to contribute to the support of children from the marriage which had been dissolved, you could not get a license to remarry unless you could prove that the remarriage would not interfere with your obligation to support your children by the first marriage. The United States Supreme Court said that the law was unconstitutional because it violated the fundamental right to marry.

Again, in a case brought against the U.S. Department of Agriculture, the Department of Agriculture had a provision in its food stamp program which required that for a household to be eligible to get food stamps it would have to be composed of individuals who were related by blood or by marriage or by adoption. A lower federal court said that the Department's regulation was unconstitutional on the ground that recent Supreme Court decisions made it clear that even the states, which possess a general police power not granted to Congress, cannot in the name of morality infringe the rights to privacy and freedom of association in the home. So your right to live with someone who is not a relative and to whom you are not married, and get food stamps, is now a basic constitutional right. When this decision was appealed to the U.S. Supreme Court, it simply upheld the decision of the lower court, saying that a restriction based on marriage was wholly without any rational basis. This again has a rather serious effect on the basic institution of society.

Finally, two states, New Jersey and Alabama, had passed laws restricting welfare benefits to married couples with dependent children. When these were contested in court, the Supreme Court said that marriage had nothing to do with eligibility for welfare benefits, because this is denying the dependent children the equal protection of the laws.

"Moral Neutrality" Imposed by the State

We are confronted with a dilemma in this country, the dilemma of pluralism. There is no denying that we are a pluralistic society. Whether it is good, bad, or indifferent, it is a massive social fact, and there is no changing it, and any suggestions for changing it into something else are simply unrealistic. Furthermore, we are a democratic society, operating on the principle of the political equality of all citizens. That means that government must treat all citizens as equals before the law. But this principle is now widely taken to mean that government must be neutral toward all beliefs and preferences. In the eyes of the law, all convictions, all moral beliefs, are mere preferences, toward which government must be neutral.

Yesterday someone came to the microphone and asked a question, the gist of which was this: "How can we have any public morality when, by the mere fact that some significant minority objects to it, it is no longer public and, therefore, government may not stand behind it?" That, I think, pinpoints the real problem posed by the drift of our constitutional law and civil rights legislation at the present time. It comes down to a systematic denial that it is possible for the United States or any state of the union to have or uphold a public morality, because that would mean that government is imposing the morality of some upon others. It is quietly assumed that it is possible for a government to be neutral on all moral questions. The result is a steady lowering of the moral sights, backed up by law, and imposed through antidiscrimination statutes. The government and, in particular, the courts are put under constant pressure to intervene actively in private institutions in order to make them neutral.

I teach in a university, and I do not think its experience is different from that of any other university. I know that we can hardly make a move in a personnel case without the threat of a lawsuit. This has a distinctively chilling effect on our decisions. Some of the decisions may indeed be bad decisions which should be chilled. But if you look at the overall effect of this constant threat of lawsuits upon the institution, it means that progressively it loses its independence.

The result is a bureaucratic state governing a flattened-out society in which people live in what Alexis de Tocqueville a hundred and fifty years ago called a "soft despotism," in which the passion for equality abolishes liberty and with it, in the long run, pluralism. What we then get is what someone else has called the universal, homogeneous administrative state.

Finally, to conclude, I will make one overall suggestion: let us start to change our thinking. I am certainly in favor of both faith and renewal, an alliance for which this conference encourages; but I would suggest that in regard to civil order, we learn to doubt. Become very skeptical of the conventional wisdom. Do not let yourself be buffaloed. Do not let yourself be talked down. Ask questions and say, "Why should we believe this?"

For example, we could begin by rethinking the individual versus the state as the necessary starting point of political theory. We could instead start with the idea, a very old one, going back as far as Aristotle, that man is a naturally social being, and naturally political, insofar as he needs, for the development of his nature, an organized society under government and law. Instead of thinking of the political order as a collection of individuals formed to protect individual rights alone, we could think of the political order as sustaining a community of communities—a new and better conception of pluralism. We could reject the notion that there is an irresolvable conflict between individual rights and public morality. I am certainly not denying or questioning the proposition that individual human beings have basic human rights. But they are *human* rights, not the right to frame your own individual conception of morality. They are rights that must fit within some overarching community order, based upon some conception of what human beings are and what is good for human beings. We could go on to make the strengthening of private institutions, the family in particular, the focus of public policy.

Suppose we were to say, "Yes, government is concerned with the welfare of all its people," but insofar as possible, it is going to pursue that welfare through strengthening, harmonizing, and if need be subsidizing private institutions that perform services of welfare to the community. Government will try especially to shore up, bolster, and strengthen the institution of the family as being the most basic transmitter of culture, of religion, and of the foundations of society.

Next, we could seek a better understanding of the phrase in the First Amendment, an "establishment of religion." The First Amendment has been in the Constitution since 1791, but interpreting that clause is really only forty years old. It dates back to the case of *Everson* v. *Board of Education* in 1947. Prior to that decision, there were only three, possibly four, decisions of the Supreme Court interpreting the meaning of an establishment of religion, because the question seldom arose at the federal level. In 1947, the Court said that nonestablishment of religion is implicit in the Fourteenth Amendment and applies on the state level. That is where the cases arise, primarily connected with schools, but with a lot of other institutions also.

Since 1947 we have a whole body of case law interpreting an establishment of religion. As Richard John Neuhaus recently remarked, and I think he is right, this is largely the handiwork of one man, Leo Pfeffer, the general counsel of the American Jewish Congress, who, somewhat to his surprise, won case after case after case before the Supreme Court. Neuhaus said it was rather astonishing that he met with so little opposition. But Neuhaus has also mentioned that evangelical groups are now going to court aggressively and bringing cases to fight to change that interpretation of establishment. If that is true, I commend them. There ought to be more of that. I find it highly unfortunate that church-state relations have had to be fought out in the courts as interpretations of the Constitution, but if that is how they must be determined, let's get into the action and fight the fight.

I would like to end with quoting something which I read every time I pass through Washington Square in New York, where there is a massive arch, the Washington Arch. And at the top, there is carved the concluding paragraph of George Washington's farewell address to the nation, the last line of which is this: "Let us erect a standard to which the wise and the good may repair. The event is in the hands of God." I think for our Christian endeavor, we may steal that line. It is for us to erect a standard, which is the cross of Christ, and hope that the wise and the good will repair to it. But we must remember that the event is in the hands of God. We are not divine providence. It is not our function to plan history and then make the plan come true. It is not within our power to save the United States. All we can do is the will of God, as God gives us to see his will and the power to carry it out, and leave the outcome in his hands. He asks for nothing more. We do not have to know how the divine plan comes out. All we have to know is the part that we are supposed to play in it. What I talked about this afternoon is a very minor part in comparison to the other things that have been talked about in this conference. But it is one small part, and some of us should get in there and play it.

FOUR

Christian Morality Adrift

J.I. Packer

M Y TITLE IS MEANT TO SUGGEST A PICTURE. Think of "Christian morality" as a compendium of truth and wisdom that contains all that is involved in defining the Christian's obedience to God—all the principles, precepts, rules, standards, prohibitions, counsels, and statements of ideal that make up God's law; all the values and virtues that God tells us to seek for ourselves and promote in the lives of others; all the subjective factors—a good conscience, a heart grateful to God, reverent love for Christ, knowledge, thoughtfulness, self-distrust, reliance on divine help—that must be there if one is going to please God. Think of this body of truth and wisdom as a ship crossing the waters of this world. The place for a ship is in the sea, but, said D. L. Moody, God help the ship if the sea gets into it! That, however, is what has started to happen.

So think, now, of the good ship "Christian morality" as drifting off course. Up on the bridge a crowd of people has been squabbling as to which of them should steer, with the result that the ship is not being effectively steered at all. It has already grazed some rocks and started to leak, and unless remedial action is taken (which will involve sorting out the confusions on the bridge) its condition is bound to get worse. God will no doubt ensure that it does not sink altogether, for if it did his promise of perpetual preservation for his church and his truth till Christ comes again would have failed. But the battering that Christian morality has received in this century, among both Protestants and Roman Catholics, has already done much harm.

Recently I saw in a leading Anglican weekly a pathetic letter from a man who said that if the church had taken a clear line about the unlawfulness of homosexual connections, his clergyman friend who had just died of AIDS might have been alive still. Let that "if" haunt your mind and sear your heart as you recall that a century ago, in a pre-Freudian era, all the churches of Christendom did take such a line, and buggery was an indictable offence in both Britain and America. But the world slipped from its earlier standards at this point, as it has at so many other points, and Christian morality has slipped with it. That is the situation we face today. My aim in this essay is to try to achieve some in-depth understanding of what has happened, with a view to seeing what needs to be said and done about it by those who think the old paths of faith and life were right and deviations from them are wrong.

Our first step must be to get clear, if we can, on the fundamental structure of Christian morality—a matter on which, as I think you will agree, clarity is often lacking. I shall therefore give some attention to presenting a scheme which seems to me to catch what is essential regarding both the material and the method of Christian moral thought.

The Nature of Christian Morality

1. **Christian morality is an expression, function, and corollary of Christian *theology*.** Our ethics are to be drawn from our *dogmatics*, and our view of both our ethics and our dogmatics will be deficient if we fail to see this. Christian morality is not to be equated with secular morality, or the morality of a national cultural heritage; Christian duty is determined by Christian doctrine; orthopraxy, as we may call it, follows from, and is controlled and shaped by, orthodoxy. Nor should any statement of Christian orthodoxy be thought of as complete till it includes a declaration of God's will for human behavior, which is what Christian morality is about. Christian morality is precisely the doctrine of God's commands to mankind, set within the frame of the doctrines of his works for mankind and his ways with mankind. God the creator, the God of the Bible, wants his human creatures to serve, please, and glorify him by specific types

and courses of action that he likes to see, and he directs us accordingly, with sanctions to encourage us to do right and to discourage us from doing wrong. Christian morality, according to Scripture, is a blueprint for living under the authority of this awesomely and intrusively personal Lord, by whose grace we have been saved to serve, and to whom we must one day give account. So Christian morality is a morality of divine command, based on the reality of a divine gift, and both the gift and the command are elements in the doctrine of God as such. Ethics, therefore, must never be thought of as independent of dogmatics, and study in either of these fields should be understood as obligating study in the other one as well. Otherwise, ultimate inadequacy in our chosen field, whichever of the two it is, becomes a foregone conclusion.

2. **Christian morality is an expression, function, and index of Christian spirituality**, that is, of the believer's whole life of communion with God by grace. The practice of Christian morality, which is the outward aspect of living the Christian life, must never be separated in thought, let alone in reality, from the inward aspect of that life—by which I mean such things as the exercise of conscience, the prayers for help, the joy of obedience, the grateful love of God, the active hoping for heaven, the cherishing of a sense of Christ's presence with us, and the constant battling against temptation, depression, apathy, and hardness of heart, which you may call sloth or accidie, if you like old names.

If our thoughts about doing God's will get detached from our thoughts about the inner spiritual life, as if these were two areas of reality and not one, or if—even worse—we define the Christian life entirely in terms of external obedience and forget that there is more to it than mechanically correct performance, then we can hardly avoid ending up in some version of legalistic Pharisaism, in which all the emphasis is on what we do rather that what we are, and into which the reality of Christian freedom does not enter. Then, like the Jews of Paul's day, we shall be rightly accused of going around to establish our own works-righteousness, and of lacking proper acquaintance with the Christ whose saving grace is for sinners only. In the deepest sense Christian morality—the morality of faith, hope, and love, pursued with discretion, self-control, fair-mindedness and courage— is not Christian at all save as it is set in this evangelical context and made to rest on the truth that Christ's servants live only by being daily forgiven for their daily failures. We forget this at our peril; but a resolve to observe the connection between our morality and our spirituality will help us to remember it.

The Norms of Christian Morality

Under the heading of norms of Christian morality, I have three points to make. They are substantial and weighty, and basic to the view of things that I wish to offer, so please be patient as I plod my way through them.

1. **All the norms of Christian morality are both *revealed* and *rational*.** As revealed, they are matters of divine command; as rational, they are embodiments of human wisdom; and there is no conflict between the morality of authentic revelation and authentic reason at any point. Let me explain.

Christianity is a revealed religion, and the Bible, which from one point of view is an explanatory record of God's revelation in history, in the process that found its climax in Christ and his church, is from another point of view God's revelation in writing. Epistemologically (that is, for the purpose of gaining knowledge), revelation is the fundamental Christian fact, and recognition of the Bible as the ultimate source and criterion of truth is basic to Christian theological method. None of us, I trust, will quarrel with that, even if Catholic, Protestant, and Orthodox have to beg leave of each other to spell out this position in slightly different ways. Nor, I trust, will anyone quarrel with me when I go on to say that the biblical writers themselves affirm the universality of a "natural" or "general" revelation that no rational being in God's world is able to evade, namely a revelation of God as the creator who ought to be worshiped and the judge who will one day call everyone to account, and of the standards that theology describes as God's *natural law* for human life.

Paul is most forthright about this in Romans 1:18-2:16, the main part of the first section of his argument in that letter, in which he diagnoses all mankind, Jew and Gentile alike, as being hopelessly guilty of sin against their maker and so as standing helplessly under his wrath. God's wrath, as Paul and indeed all Scripture conceives it, is his characteristic judicial hostility to sin. God, says Paul, is already showing his wrath by letting sin have its head and breed more sin, and one day he will show that same wrath by catastrophic retribution upon all of sinning mankind. Through the agency of Jesus Christ as judge, pronouncing sentence, there will on that day be "tribulation and distress for every soul of man who does evil, of the Jew first and also of the Greek" (2:9). All deserve such treatment, for all have sinned against moral knowledge that they actually have. None will be able to plead ignorance of the law for breaking which they are condemned. Paul thus founds Christianity's claim to be the universal religion for humanity on the fact that it alone—perhaps I had better say, Christ alone—offers rescue from the wrath-provoking guilt that is humanity's universal predicament.

How does Paul make his point about the universality of moral knowledge? By the following line of reasoning. God's wrath, he says, is "revealed from heaven" (revealed, that is, first in mankind's spiritual and moral downhill slide, then in each person's bad conscience, and then in the gospel message, as the ongoing context makes plain) against all human failure to worship and obey him (1:18). These failures are guilty because they flow from willful suppression and distortion of knowledge that everyone is given of God as creator and source of all good (1:19-23). God in reaction has removed restraints on the manifold immoralities that humans do in fact crave to practice (1:24-31). Consciences, however, remain alive, so that all human beings have inward inklings that "those who practice such things are worthy of death" even while they themselves do them and applaud others who do them (1:32). Proof of the universality of these God-given inklings, even where no biblical instruction has ever been received, lies in the reality of pagan moral experience: "When the Gentiles who do not have the law do instinctively the things of the law, these, not having the law, are a law to themselves, in that they show the work of the law written on their hearts, their conscience bearing witness, and their thoughts alternately accusing or else defending them" (2:14 f). In other words, all mankind, however pagan and uninstructed, knows what it is to do some things that God's word shows to be really right, and to do those things because they are known to be right, and to have a good conscience for doing them and a bad conscience for omitting them.

What is contained in this universally revealed divine law? Paul's argument specifies, first, grateful worship of the sovereign creator (1:21) and, second, the opposite of all those types of action that Paul says people know to be "worthy of death" (1:32) even while they engage in them. The list of these types of action is grim, but we had better hear it so as to be sure we know what Paul is talking about. It starts with what is nowadays called same-sex loving on the part of both women and men, and goes on to cover "all unrighteousness, wickedness, greed, evil, . . . envy, murder, strife, deceit, malice" whereby people become "gossips, slanderers, haters of God, insolent, arrogant, boastful, inventors of evil, disobedient to parents, without understanding, untrustworthy, unloving, unmerciful" (1:26-31). It is the opposite of these categories of conduct and character that the natural law, the law of our creation, prescribes. From this it becomes apparent that God's supernatural verbal revelation from heaven of the kinds of behavior that he loves and hates to see, the revelation, I mean, of divine standards in the Decalogue and in the moral teaching of the prophets, the apostles, and the Lord himself, is fundamentally nothing more, just as it is nothing less, than republication, confirmation, and reinforcement of the natural law that the world in a fashion knows already, but is resolved to ignore.

Empirical evidence goes far to confirm this contention. As C.S. Lewis showed in a striking appendix to his book *The Abolition of Man,* the "Tao" (as he called it) of social righteousness according to the biblically revealed law of God has in fact been articulated by authoritative moral teachers in all developed cultures. Lewis's evidence indicates that in one milieu after another this part of the natural law surfaces spontaneously, which is what you would expect, since it is actually impressed by God through general revelation on all human hearts, however little particular individuals and groups may be willing even to try to live by it. Thus we may claim for the natural law of Romans 1 and 2, at any rate on its social side, the rationality that it is always proper to ascribe to matters of universal acknowledgment.

And a compelling case can be made for the entire natural law being rational in the further sense that it fits human nature, inasmuch as it points to the path on which the goal for which each person was made, and the ultimate contentment that each human heart craves, are actually found. The law of spiritual and social righteousness that God makes known by both natural and supernatural revelation is in truth the maker's handbook for humanity, of which we may and must say what has sometimes to be said of other makers' handbooks also—"if all else fails"—rather, *when* all else fails—*"read the instructions!"* God's law, understood teleologically as setting out values, virtues, and behavior patterns to aim at, and limits within which to stay, suits and benefits us by delineating to us what constitutes our own true fulfillment. Abraham Maslow was not wrong to celebrate self-fulfillment, or self-realization, as a happy condition; he was only wrong in his analysis of it, and his ideas about the way to it. The true path here is the path of keeping God's commandments in the world of relationship to God and others that is ours. This is the path from which sin diverts us, and to which grace restores us. It leads us into the happy worship and devotion on the one hand, and the practice of love and justice and joy in human relationships on the other, that between them constitute our glorifying of God. And as we thus glorify God, fulfillment, contentment, and realization of who and what we are in terms of God's wise plan for us become increasingly ours.

Today's unbelieving world, which has no conception of fellowship with God and no adequate idea of human nature anyway, may well deny all this out of hand as ridiculous, and I suspect that here on earth we Christians do not know enough about our own identity and nature before God to see the full reason why, for instance, the law of God should tie us to heterosexual relations within marriage, and socially to the preservation of human life in all its forms even when this means sacrificing personal convenience. Yet I think that thoughtful Christians are able to see enough of the overall effect on character of staying within these limits on the one hand, and of refusing to stay within them on the other, to argue effectively in any company for the intrinsic rationality of God's revealed norms, just as they have been doing since Christianity began. And when the argument is made, thoughtful unbelievers, even those who fight against it, cannot but acknowledge that it has real substance.

So much, then, for the dual character of the norms of Christian morality as both revealed and rational. I move now to my second point.

2. **All the norms of Christian morality are both** *creational* **and** *covenantal.* My thesis is that God's commands in the natural law, which the Decalogue restates and the New Testament moral teaching embodies, always remain the same in essence, for they are rooted in the realities of creation; although within that basic frame there appear angles, applications, and additions that are determined by the stage that God's gracious covenant purpose for his own needy people has reached at any one time. I affirm this core continuity of God's law against all versions of the idea that Old and New Testament moralities are in direct opposition, or that the latter grew out of the former by some form of evolutionary development, or that the so-called "kingdom ethics" of the New Testament are meant to replace, rather than reinforce, the "creation ethics" of the Old Testament era. The basic moral norms for mankind are not arbitrary enactments on God's part, but are determined by two unchanging facts. The first fact is the goodness and holiness of the divine creator, which we are all called to acknowledge by gratefully seeking to please him. The second fact is the nature of the human creature, whose capacity for freedom and contentment is only ever fulfilled through actively loving and serving God and others. It is true that some of the deeper dimensions of these norms are only seen by the light of the full Christian revelation; for instance, only when God is known as a triune fellowship of holy love, into which we hell-bent humans are brought by sovereign grace alone, can the relational implications of loving God and others as God loves us be adequately grasped. Nonetheless, the norms as such, in relatively firm outline, are already revealed to mankind in and through our very existence as God's creatures in his world. And the identity in all ages of these basic norms, whether known through general revelation apart from Scripture or through the special, supernatural, verbal, historically contextualized revelation given in the Mosaic law and in the law of Christ, must be maintained, it seems to me, as a vital step towards clear thinking about Christian morality in this or any day.

How then are we to account for the differences that the Bible itself specifies between the Old and New Testament morality? The answer is: by drawing two distinctions. The first is the distinction between on the one hand the kinds of actions, defined in terms of behavior towards God, one's neighbor, and oneself, that God's law requires and forbids, and that should therefore be seen as matters of divine command to all human beings as such, and on the other hand the special motivations of faith that arise from the realities of God's gracious covenant relationship, and that are therefore required only of those whom God has actually taken into that relationship. This distinction is crucial in itself, and very clarifying to the mind; let me illustrate what it means.

The first table of the Decalogue, as set out in Deuteronomy 5:6-15 and summarized in the *Shema* of 6:4-5, which Jesus identified as the first and great commandment (Mt 22:35-38), states a motive for worshiping the creator that applied only to Israel, namely, that the creator is also Yahweh, their covenant God, who redeemed them from Egyptian bondage. Romans 1:21, however, indicates that since all humans should be aware that they owe to God all the good they have ever received, starting with their very existence, grateful worship is a duty. This is implied also by Peter's statement to Cornelius that in every nation those who revere God and do what is right gain his favor (Acts 10:35)—a statement that can hardly be limited to the category of first-century God-fearers (Gentile fellow-travellers with Jews) to which Cornelius belonged, nor be invalidated by our total uncertainty as to whether the class of human beings who truly worship the creator on the basis of general revelation alone has nowadays any members. The point I am illustrating is simply that a type of action that is universally commanded on the basis of creation may be linked in God's economy with a further motive that is drawn from God's redeeming work; which can, however, be required only of the particular human group that God's redemption and covenant commitment have actually embraced.

Thus covenantal considerations, founded on the realities of redemption, do in fact yield additional motives—reasons, we would say—for observing the common principles of creational morality. Particular motives drawn by God's command from saving grace are to be consciously superimposed on universal motives deriving from creation and providence by those to whom that saving grace has come. All mankind should be worshiping and serving the creator out of gratitude for creation, and believers should be worshiping and serving out of gratitude for redemption as well. Right motivation is a matter of divine command, just as right action is, but right motivation for Christians today, as for Jews of the Old Testament time, involves more than is required of persons who are as yet

ignorant of God's redemptive action. Recognition of this difference—recognition, that is, that the correct theological answers to
the question "why should I do such-and-such?" have differed for
different groups at different times in world history—seems to me to
be another vital step towards clear thinking about Christian morality,
though it is not possible to draw out the full implications of it here.

So far I have been speaking of behavioral commands that belong to
the law of creation, Lewis's "Tao," and that therefore remain
identical throughout human history. But now comes a second
distinction that we must draw. Just as new specific motives for
obeying this natural law flow from the facts of redemption and
covenant, so new specific divine commands to particular communities rest on these same facts. To demonstrate this, I now list the
main differences between God's commands under the Mosaic
dispensation (the old covenant) and the Christian order of things
(the new covenant). Under the former, much of the divinely
instituted pattern of life and worship was typical, temporary, and
designed specifically to educate God's covenant people to understand Christ when he came. Under the latter, the kingdom of God
and life in the Spirit, foretasting heaven, are realities, and God's
education of his covenant people has the hope of heaven's full joy as
its new focus. Out of the progression from the one dispensation to
the other came the following changes in the specifics of God's
command to human beings in the realm of what is commonly called
his positive, as distinct from his natural, law:

• The typical priesthood, sacrificial system, liturgical calendar,
and purity regulations of Old Testament worship were fulfilled,
transcended, replaced, and abolished by the mediatorial action of
Jesus Christ, which in one way or another they foreshadowed.
Therefore God's old covenant commands concerning these things
are no longer in force for anyone.

• The national life of Israel, with its home and foreign policy and
internal legal system determined in the first instance by Mosaic
legislation, was superseded by the international life of the Christian
church, which is not one of this world's nations at all. Thus Mosaic
legislation relating to Israel's national life ceases to have any direct
application as God's command to particular persons or groups, and
God no longer instructs his people to act as executioners of his

judgment on his enemies by holy war, as he did on occasion in Old Testament times (compare Romans 12:19).

• The Old Testament promises of material blessing for faithfulness, which had typical significance and an educational role, have been replaced by promises of endless glory at Christ's parousia and warnings to expect recurring tribulation until then. The hope of heaven, of being "for ever with the Lord," has new prominence and new force as a motive to holiness (compare 1 John 3:2f), as compared with the hints dropped about it in the Old Testament writings.

• Christ requires Christians to distinguish between the divorce procedure that God permitted and tolerated under Moses and the creation ideal of lifelong monogamous marriage, and to recognize willful divorce, with subsequent remarriage, as action that he does not favor (compare Matthew 19:1-9; 5:31f; Luke 16:18).

• Obedience under the Christian dispensation has been given a Christocentric and Christological focus: God commands Christians to imitate the love, humility, and entire moral character of their master out of gratitude for his saving mercy and out of loyalty to him as their Lord, and correlates this command with the revelation that the indwelling Holy Spirit is actively transforming them even now into the likeness of the risen Lord to whom they are united (2 Cor 3:18, etc.). The Christlikeness that is commanded, and that Christians must therefore labor to practice, is achieved, insofar as it is achieved, by the enabling power of the Holy Spirit.

• Christians, though consciously free from the typical and dispensational restrictions of the Jewish law with regard to the use and enjoyment of created things, are to be guided in using this liberty by the following explicit principles, all reflecting the new reality of personal and corporate life in Christ: They are not to do what their own conscience is uncertain about (Rom 14:23), nor to press others to do what their consciences are uncertain about (Rom 14:13-20; 1 Cor 8), nor to induce addictions that enslave them (1 Cor 6:12). These apostolic injunctions have the status of divine commands, given for the new situation to ensure that Christian liberty is not abused.

• Divine commands to use the Christian sacraments (Mt 28:19; 1 Cor 11:25), to respect and provide for Christian presbyters (1 Cor 16:16; Gal 6:6; 1 Thess 5:12; Heb 13:17; 1 Pt 5:5), and to show special love to Christians as such, as fellow-siblings in God's family (1 Cor 13:34f; Gal 6:2, 10; etc.), have replaced comparable Old Testament commandments regarding circumcision and Passover, provisions for priests, and the special obligations of Israelites to help each other.

All these specific changes in God's commands to men follow directly from the way in which his plan of world redemption has advanced beyond the era of Old Testament anticipations to that of New Testament fulfillment. But this law of Christ for his redeemed people should still be seen as meshing with the natural law to supplement its contents, and as focusing the frame of reference within which Christians must pursue the purposes and policies of love and justice that the natural law requires of them. The natural law remains the basis on which all that is distinctive in Christian morality is superimposed.

Now to the third point, which completes the picture.

3. All the norms of Christian morality are both *regulational* and *relational*. What I mean by this is that these norms are not abstractions but are commands of God that bear directly on all aspects of our living, and that under God we learn what they contain and how they bear on us not simply by applying moral universals to particular cases, but also by discerning the values and claims that are built into relationships. God's regulations determine the substance of right action, viewed as obedience, but it is relational awareness that imparts to right actions its temper and quality as love. And because this is so, full perception of these norms requires not only our analytical reasoning powers but also an empathetic use of our creative imagination within our relationships. This use, however, will only ever be sparked effectively when the motive of love is operating in us already in some shape or form.

In saying this, I extend the use of the word "norms" beyond what I think is usual nowadays, to include in its meaning the exercise and expression of Christian virtue, or the graces of Christian character, as the older Protestant theology would have put it, along with the divinely commanded classes of actions of which I have been speaking so far. I make this extension because reality so requires. I am saying that "be a certain sort of person" is, formally speaking, as much a Christian, and indeed a human, moral norm as is "do these certain things." I am affirming (and surely this is no new teaching!) that both natural law and biblical revelation require specific attitudes and dispositions, as well as specific actions and habits. In the abstract, ideal virtue, that is, virtue of character in fullest manifestation, is a moral norm in itself no less than observance of the commands and limits of God's law is a moral norm. And in Christianity according to the word of God, the personal perfection of Jesus Christ is the ultimate norm and model for all moral action, which norm is only properly described by saying that here in Jesus you have perfect conformity to God's law as the foundation, with fully manifested virtue as the superstructure. But it was the love-relation of the incarnate Son to the Father, and to humankind for the Father's sake, that brought his moral virtue into the empathetic, imaginative expression that really constituted the normative quality of his obedience, and it is to imitating this, over and above committing and restricting ourselves to divinely approved types of actions, that we who are Christians are called. Let me illustrate.

First illustration: Jesus told the story of the Good Samaritan to teach a lawyer the universal scope of the moral norm of neighbor-love. "That every person you meet, no matter how uncongenial, is your needy neighbor whom you must help if you can" is the regulational norm that he enunciates. But the story itself is of ideal, empathetic, imaginative neighbor-love, that is, of unlimited goodwill and readiness to sacrifice convenience, time, and resources in order to help a stranger, and we can only ever expect such gestures of creative kindness to be called forth in real life by a prior relational reality, namely love to a loving God (think of Mother Teresa). When, however, Jesus says, "Go and do the same" (Luke 10:27), he makes the Samaritan's spirit and style of action part of the norm; and such a norm, as everyone can see, goes far beyond the merely regulational.

Second illustration: Jesus, who was himself, of course, the archetype of the Good Samaritan in his own story, was confronted by a group of hostile Jewish theologians who apparently had just surprised a couple in the act of adultery. They brought the woman (not the man, note), and they "set her in the midst" in order then to ask Jesus whether he thought the Mosaic directive to stone adulterers should be applied in her case. (It was one of those catch questions to which it was expected that any answer would discredit Jesus with somebody, in this case either the Jewish community or the Roman authorities, who would not allow the Jews to inflict the death penalty.) Jesus first stooped down, deliberately taking his eyes off the woman, and wrote on the ground, thus indicating that the theologians' question was fit only to be ignored. Then, as it was pressed, he said, "He who is without sin among you, let him be the first to throw a stone at her" (Jn 8:7), and wrote on the ground again, as if to dismiss the matter. When the theologians, stunned and shamed, had quietly vanished, Jesus faced the adulteress for the first time and told her simply that he was not there at that moment as a judge to condemn her; she was to go, and not sin that way again.

What amazing behavior! And what creative, compassionate utterance on the savior's part! Jesus' sensitivity to the woman's inescapable feelings of guilt, fear, humiliation, and being destroyed by men, linked with such ingenuity in stymieing the theologians' malice to them both, in avoiding any further contribution to the woman's hurt, and in communicating forgiveness to her in the way best calculated to renew self-respect and so make psychologically possible a new start, is in truth breathtaking. It displays a degree of wise and creative benevolence, springing from desire for another person's human and spiritual well-being, that the world never saw, nor dreamed of, until Jesus showed it. And this imaginative ingenuity, triggered by love, goes far beyond formal regulational correctness. Jesus here expresses, and so models for us, his followers, a quality of spontaneous good will to God's human image-bearers that we can only ever enter into at all as a by-product, overflowing from our own responsive love-relation to the Father and the Son, who have so greatly and amazingly loved us. It is in this sense that the normative attitude and outlook (as distinct from the motivation) of our Christian lives is to be derived, partly at least, from our relation to God—which is the point I am here concerned to give substance.

Such, then, as I see it, in simple though not, I hope, simplistic terms, is the essential structure (maybe I should say substructure) of biblical Christian morality, in which the law of nature is also a matter of divine command, and God's commands make human sense as the means of leading us in righteousness to glorify and enjoy our Savior-God, which is the goal and fulfillment of human life. It would be very satisfying to round off this overview with a study of how the Holy Spirit enables Christians to obey God's law and through that obedience transforms them into some measure of moral likeness to Christ, but that cannot be done now; we have to move on.

What Undermines Christian Moral Thought Today

In light of our analysis we can now get clear on what has happened in modern times to send Christian morality off course. Three things call for mention, and the first is:

1. **The erosion of Christian supernaturalism.** This has been a problem particularly within Protestantism. Christian morality, so we said, is a department of dogmatics; orthopraxy flows from orthodoxy, and damage to our dogmatics is bound to mean that our ethics suffer too. This being so, it is ominous to observe how for almost two centuries Protestant dogmatics have been undergoing major damage from the rationalistic antisupernaturalism that was begotten and bred up in the Enlightenment, found its home among Lutheran scholars in German universities, and is now entrenched, under the question-begging label of Liberalism, in many theological teaching institutions both sides of the Atlantic. Risky and odious as generalizations are, I think I may fairly offer a generic profile of it as follows.

Enlightenment theology conceives God in a unitarian rather than a trinitarian way, and denies that he communicates with us in language, or that he judges mankind for sins, or that he acts to redeem us in any other sense than by presiding over, or perhaps directing from within, the religious and cultural evolution of our race. Some of this is deism negating theism, and some of it is immanentism rejecting deism, but there is full agreement that the theistic supernaturalism of the historic trinitarian and incarnational faith must be rejected, and so it is. Process theology, calling itself pantheism and affirming the finitude of God, is the latest form of this rejection.

Against its unitarian background, Enlightenment theology develops non-incarnational Christologies that see Jesus as an ideal religious and prophetic figure from whom we can learn, rather than a divine Lord by whom we must be saved, and that combine confidence that he did not die as a sacrifice for our sins with doubt as to whether he rose from the dead and whether the world will ever see him again.

As for the Bible, it is not in any sense a record and embodiment of revealed truth, for on Enlightenment principles there is no such thing. The Bible is, rather, a library of Judaeo-Christian classics, a treasury of religious thought and feeling over a period of something like a thousand years. It links insight with superstition and false history with true in a bewildering way that, fortunately, clever scholars can now sort out.

What was the effect of all this on Christian morals? At first, less than you might have expected. The deist thinker Kant, architect of the Liberal denial of verbal revelation, who has often (God save us!) been called the philosopher of Protestantism, was a moralist who maintained the reality of ethical absolutes in the form of the categorical imperative and identified many of the absolutes correctly by biblical standards. The idea that the church's job is to set up on earth the kingdom of God, viewed as a Kantian "kingdom of ends" (that is, a state of society in which each person is valued as an end rather than a means), soon gripped Liberal hearts, as indeed with some rephrasing it grips them still. To typical Liberals Christianity was in essence, as they liked to put it, the ethic of the Sermon on the Mount, and they served their vision of moral people in a moral society with great zeal.

However, toward the end of the nineteenth century evolutionism came to dominate many Western minds, encouraging the belief that in culture and morals generally whatever is, is right, because it is the latest product of the evolutionary process. This inclined the practitioners of Enlightenment theology, which by then had exchanged Kantian deism for Hegelian immanentism as its characteristic philosophical outlook, to give up any notion of unchanging natural law and instead treat any latter-day community consensus as a revelation of the present will of God. That tendency led most German Liberals to support the militarism of two world wars, as it now leads most North American Liberals to support violence in the service of social change and to condone abortion, on the grounds, it seems, that you can meaningfully affirm the value of your neighbor, the pregnant woman, by killing at her request your other neighbor who is currently housed inside her. Also, Liberal denials of verbal revelation make an ethic of divine command impossible, and oblige you to re-categorize biblical ethics as the fruit of human religious insight long ago, insight that is in principle relative to and open to question by the alleged insight of later generations. Thus the entire structure of Christian morality, as I have analyzed it, is undermined. So I conclude that the long-term effect of Protestant Liberalism on Christian morals will continue to be, as it already has been, unhappy.

2. The assimilation of secular moral perspectives. This has become a vice of method in both Protestantism and Roman Catholicism in recent years. The reason is not far to seek. The post-Christian drift of the twentieth century has put Christian morality under great and sustained pressure. The cultural optimism with which the century opened was deflated by the First World War, and since then the prevalent mood of the West has been one of practical materialism and egoistic hedonism, fed by what Freud is supposed to have taught about the unhealthiness of sexual restraint. American pragmatism and European positivism have joined hands to create an atmosphere unfavorable to any moral absolutes, and in relation to our educational and cultural establishments historic Christianity has been comprehensively marginalized. If, under these circumstances, persons who want to make Christianity sound relevant borrow the world's own thoughts in order then to present them to the world as Christian truth, it may make us sad, but it should come as no surprise. In fact, it has happened already, and will no doubt go on happening, over and over again.

At first the Roman Catholic Church stood resolutely aloof from Protestant Liberalism, and gave the parallel Modernist movement in its own ranks short shrift. But Vatican II was thought to sanction revisionist experiments, and one such, in the moral realm, has been the embracing of the view called consequentialism. Its central thesis corresponds to that proposed to Protestants by Joseph Fletcher in his well-known book *Situation Ethics* (1966), namely, that there is only ever one criterion to apply for determining what it is right to do, and that criterion is the comparing of the likely consequences of the possible lines of action.

When I took moral philosophy in the 1940's, this procedure was called using the utilitarian calculus, which secular moralists have been debating for more than a hundred years. The thought behind it was, and for consequentialists still is, that no act is intrinsically evil, nor yet intrinsically good: only its consequences give it either quality. An obvious corollary is that, if the calculation of consequences so directs, it will become right to do what others, thinking in different terms, will regard as evil in order that good may come.

An obvious objection is that no publicly agreed version of the calculus can ever be established, because it is a fundamental fact about humankind that different people estimate the relative worth of particular good things—values, as we would say—differently; so any assessment of the quantity of good involved in each particular set of consequences is inescapably subjective or disputable.

But the overwhelming objection, in light of my argument so far, is that consequentialism, from the word go, ignores God's revealed commands in Scripture, and in the natural law as Scripture enables us to recognize that law. What God commands, in the first instance, is not that we calculate consequences across the board in order to determine what is good and bad (in fact, consequences only become relevant when we are choosing between equally legitimate options); what he commands, rather, is that we observe and honor his own prior determinations of what is good and bad, that is, his teaching about the kinds of actions that he loves or hates to see, and that make for or against the fulfillment of our created human nature. Consequentialism has found eloquent advocates in Roman Catholicism in recent years, but, because it cuts loose from God's law, natural and revealed, it must be judged an egregious mistake.

One more unsettling factor for Christian morality remains to be mentioned, albeit briefly.

3. The prevalence of Romantic anthropology. The Romantic movement in European culture at the end of the eighteenth century threw up the dazzling ideal of the human individual as a pioneering hero, breaking all bonds of conventionality as he rises to unprecedented heights of achievement. Whereas the Englightenment begot cool, destructive skeptics, Romanticism produced passionate, creative rebels. Byron, Beethoven, Goethe, Wagner, and Nietzsche may be cited as archetypal exponents and embodiments of this ideal, and it is apparent that in a rather more trivial, lowbrow, and petulant form it has entrenched itself in the modern Western mentality. Human freedom and creativity are constantly celebrated, and voices from the existentialist camp are raised again and again to assure us that we shall never become real persons till we start to express these qualities in patterns of living that are entirely ours, learned from no one, devised entirely by following our own inner impulses. You must do your own thing, we are told: that's the only way to go.

One by-product of this mentality is that all thought of having to live under the rule of a law that has transcendent sanctions—a law, therefore, that it is beyond man's power to change—carries strongly negative vibrations. Boundaries, we feel, are for crossing, rules for breaking, locked doors for knocking down. This is the romantic hero syndrome, in its modern mutation—an anthropological Titanism, if ever there was one. Jean-Paul Sartre, himself an existentialist, complicated the scene by arguing that there is no such thing as human nature, but that our personal humanity is entirely what we make it out of the unformed raw material of potentialities that we find within ourselves. Small wonder, then, that utterance, from whatever quarter, declaring that, for instance, male and female homosexuality are contrary to nature, so that these alternative life styles are actually pathological freaks, fall on deaf ears. Our culture conditions us to want to be bounds-breaking heroes, and life within limits is dismissed as a servile and unworthy goal.

What we really have here is the I-play-God mentality of the first sin, in Eden, now reappearing in fashionable modern dress. Romantic anthropology, as such, is one of the many forms that original sin takes. By diagnosing it, however, we do not cure it, and as long as our culture, in both pop and sophisticated forms, lends it such thorough-going support as it does at present, it will continue to be an enormous obstacle to restoring any sense of the naturalness of the natural law, and the authority of the biblical ethic (the two, as I said earlier, are really one) to our benighted society. Many in our churches, quite apart from those outside them, are so intoxicated with this current cultural moonshine that they would deprecate any attempt to return to the time-honored moral standards. Nothing less, however, can help our churches or our society back to the strengths of sanity. I say sanity because in its revolt against the law of God the Western world is more or less mad, and to the extent that the churches follow the world in this, they are mad too. And the prognosis for such madness is grim.

Declared Jeremiah: "Thus says the Lord. 'Stand by the ways and see and ask for the ancient paths, where the good way is, and walk in it; and you shall find rest for your souls.' But they said, 'We will not walk in it.' And I set watchmen over you, saying, 'Listen to the sound of the trumpet.' But they said, 'We will not listen.' Therefore hear, O nations . . . hear, O earth; behold, I am bringing disaster on this people, the fruit of their plans, because they have not listened to my words, and as for my law, they have rejected it also" (Jer 6:16-19).

May it not be irrevocably so in modern North America. Lord, have mercy! Amen.

Now let me sum up in question and answer form some of the lessons that have begun to appear through our argument.

Why, we ask, as we face today's moral landslide in Western society, do our churches fail so spectacularly to be clear, strong, and united in affirming biblical moral absolutes? In terms of our opening illustration, why is there so much disagreement about how to steer the Christian moral ship? The reason is that many of the steersmen, official and otherwise, have been infected with the cancerous moral relativism that post-Christian secularity has spawned. Those whose handling of the Bible is determined by secular frames of reference do not find moral absolutes in it.

How then shall we draw from the Bible the moral absolutes that pre-twentieth-century Christians found there? First, by categorizing its explicit teaching as didactic revelation from God; second by linking it with the equally explicit teaching of universally intuited natural law.

But how, in today's skeptical world, can we give credibility to the claim that these standards of holiness make for man's highest good? By exhibiting them as the divinely revealed and empirically verified truth about the way of living that fulfills human nature, and by celebrating the power that the risen Christ through the Holy Spirit gives to practice total self-denial and self-giving that this way of life demands. (The reality of that power has also been empirically verified; think again of Mother Teresa.)

Finally, is it realistic to expect our culture to swing back to the Christian morality that it so badly needs? This can only happen as the historic gospel of Jesus Christ, the message of ruin, redemption, and regeneration, bears fruit in new lives and changed purposes. Commitment to Christian morals is a path of wisdom and duty that only Christians can be expected to understand, and ordinarily it comes as the fruit not of apologetic argument but of saving faith. So, while getting standards of conduct in the churches straight again and witnessing to our contemporaries about the way of righteousness are important, prayer for, and work in, Christian evangelism remains our prime task. It is thus that we most truly serve the world.

FIVE

An Orthodox Response to J.I. Packer

Stanley Samuel Harakas

FIRST AND FOREMOST, I want to affirm how much I appreciate the paper of Professor James I. Packer. It is a fundamentally accurate description of our times and spiritual and moral condition as a nation. I appreciate it as one who serves his church as a teacher of Eastern Orthodox Christian ethics. And I appreciate it as a believer, who with genuine pain and hurt has observed the rapid deterioration of the spiritual and moral standards of this nation. I appreciate it as a citizen of the United States, a nation to which my dear parents emigrated with the heartfelt sentiment that America was in truth, "God's country."

My remarks will be based on these four "appreciations": (1) the accuracy of the description of our situation by Dr. Packer; (2) an assessment of Dr. Packer's "divine command" ethics from an Eastern Orthodox position; (3) a painful Greek Orthodox assessment of the causes of our present situation; and (4) a prescription for what ought to be done by believers now. Certainly, a formidable agenda for such a short presentation, so of necessity my points will be made directly and simply.

1. **Packer's accuracy of description.** Dr. Packer is an astute observer of both the moral scene (that is, how Americans are actually behaving) and the ethical scene (that is, how Americans are justifying how they are behaving). He has described accurately a new situation for Americans. The original title of his paper as announced, "Biblical vs. Modernist Approaches to Morality," implied not much more than a comparison of two approaches to ethics. However, his paper now has another title, "Christian Morality Adrift." It describes not only a nation which is directionless, but also a large segment of the Christian church which is floating around on a sea of ethical relativism, and which apparently has cut the rope which has up to now held its anchor. Both America and much of the Christian church, indeed, seem to be morally and ethically adrift.

I have no quarrel with this assessment. There is no need to catalogue the extent of the moral "drifting" taking place in the societies of the Western world, and the Western hemisphere in particular. Were my response to be much longer, I would be able to show the parallels between my own writings and those of Dr. Packer's paper. Suffice it to say that I agree as an Eastern Orthodox Christian ethicist that Christian ethics is rooted in Christian doctrine and spirituality, that the norms of Christianity are broad-based, revealed, and rational, that there is a foundational moral order which is discoverable in our created human nature, in conjunction with an ethic rooted in the revelation of Jesus Christ, and that Christian ethics properly includes what Dr. Packer calls "regulational" and "relational" aspects of our existence. I also agree that the present moral malaise of Western society is the result of an erosion of belief in God, a topic I will say something about below. It is also true that unfortunately the Christian churches have absorbed much of the philosophies of this age, granting them a deficient and false baptism with the name "Christian." In truth, in the place of God, we have now come to worship and serve ourselves with our whole heart, our whole soul, and our whole mind, only occasionally and selectively breaking out of our self-centeredness to serve others.

2. **An Eastern Orthodox evaluation of Packer's "divine command" ethics.** The one emphasis I have a problem with, as an Orthodox ethicist, is Dr. Packer's presentation of what has come to be called a "divine command" ethic. From the perspective of Eastern

Orthodox Christianity, the traditional and "pure" divine command approaches to ethics, such as that of Janine Idziak (*Divine Command Morality: Historical and Contemporary Readings* [Lewiston, N.Y.: Edwin Mellon Press, 1980]), present serious problems for Christian ethics. Essentially this approach to ethics says that the good, which human beings are obligated to follow, is what God commands. In substance, it does not make any difference what God commands; it is sufficient and central that God commands it, and this creates the obligation to obey what he commands. In the Orthodox perspective, this is an extreme example of what Eastern Orthodox theology calls "Western legalism." Orthodox ethics focuses much more on what God as Holy Trinity is, what human beings are by nature of their creation in God's image, and what people are to be, in communion with God and one another. In this perspective, rules and commands are, so to speak, "shorthand descriptions" of what kinds of behavior are fitting and appropriate for human beings, created in God's image, who are growing toward the fulfillment of their very humanity in Godlikeness. The Orthodox objection to divine command ethics is that this system has all the appearances of an externally imposed, arbitrary, even capricious understanding of morality.

Now, from what has been said here already, it is clear that Dr. Packer does not subscribe to this kind of view. The broad and inclusive approach which he subscribes to in his paper does not permit such an understanding. The wide-ranging perception of norms, the acceptance of a concept of natural moral law, the focus on spirituality, the acceptance of both "regulational and relational" aspects of Christian morality, all undermine an understanding of ethics which is exclusively or even primarily a law-oriented divine command ethic. By trying to present ethics in both these modes, I see an inconsistency, and I would say that the full resources of Christian teaching which he seems to want to incorporate into his understanding should lead him to temper, if not eliminate, what now appears to be an inconsistent retention of divine command language, while actually presenting a full-blown, comprehensive, coherent, and inclusive, yet not compromised, Christian ethic.

I would like to add here a few brief comments on other points in the text. First, it is not clear to me how to reconcile on the one hand the affirmation in the earlier part of the paper which seems to say that the content of both the Old Testament and the New Testament moral

law are identical, and later statements which—in addressing motives—
imply a qualitative difference between the moral teaching of the two
testaments. As an Orthodox Christian, it seems to me to be an almost
essential understanding arising from the "completing" and "ful-
filling" aspect of the New Testament in relation to the Old.

Another brief, though very important point, is the need for
Christians to ground relational affirmations in the very nature of
God, in whose image and likeness human beings are created. Eastern
Orthodox theology constantly affirms that God is a trinity of persons
in loving communion. As a community of persons, the Holy Trinity
provides for human beings a model of personhood which by its
nature demands that human beings, in order to be fully human, must
be in relationship with God and with other human beings. One could
say that the fact that God is a Trinity is an anti-individualist norm, and
is a moral standard for human beings which calls for the development
of humanity in God-likeness in terms of loving communion and
interpersonal relationships.

While I must agree with Dr. Packer that an exclusive understanding of decision-making which looks only to consequences, that
is, "consequentialism," is a distortion and an error, the consideration
of consequences as one part of a whole process is both legitimate and
necessary. It is not only in situations in which there is a deadlock,
based on other criteria, that consequences come into play. Consequences may be factors which both help create a dilemma, as well as
solve it. A careful reading of Scripture, for example, will find appeals
to consequences sometimes as the only moral justification given for
an act or a prescribed course of action.

Finally, though it is accurate to trace the present "modernist"
mindset through the centuries to Enlightenment and other philosophical mindsets, in practice today it is a popularized, vulgar, and
unconsciously adopted existentialism that guides much decision-
making in the moral sphere in our time. Individualistic self-serving
attitudes are not, of course, new to our age. But the conviction that
this attitude is not only legitimate but morally required in the face of
a meaningless universe is now a widespread presupposition for
justifying behaviors and decisions. Popularized, unconsciously
absorbed existentialism is our fundamental enemy today.

3. **The philosophy of "negation" and its consequences: "retro-
barbarism."** I am reminded by Dr. Packer's indictment of the

contemporary scene of the writings of a Greek Orthodox thinker who wrote similar assessments in the period immediately following the Second World War. Alexander Tsirindanes was one of a group of Greek Orthodox professional persons who banded together even before the end of the Nazi occupation of Greece to reflect on the causes of the war, and to look forward to a new Europe. They, too, were much concerned about the breakdown of Western civilization, its culture, religious commitment, and morality.

Tsirindanes authored a series of articles and books, some of which were published in English. One of these was titled *Toward a Christian Civilization*. Written and published in the fifties, they have a certain outdated character to them, since Tsirindanes speaks to the people of his own generation. At the same time, he seems also to have anticipated the kinds of analysis and concern summarized by the title of this conference: "A Society in Peril."

As Tsirindanes looked back on the rise of Nazism, he saw there all the root causes of moral and ethical malaise which are identified by Dr. Packer. He coined a word, to summarize this perception: "negation." Negation was a denial of the very spiritual roots of Western society. He saw negation as a sort of self-repudiation of Western society. Negation was for him a sort of foundational spiritual suicide. At its heart was the unwillingness to acknowledge God as the central reality of civilization. What Tsirindanes saw in Nazism and Fascism, he also saw in Marxism and Leninism on the left, and increasingly in the Western capitalist societies, as well. He did believe that there was a residue of healthy faith in the West, which could be reclaimed and reintroduced into the whole range of artistic, literary, social, political, and religious life. But he did not think that this would or could come automatically.

What makes Tsirindanes even more interesting is that he related the negation of the foundational trust and belief in God, and the spiritual perspectives that that creates for every aspect of personal and social life, with the consequences so dramatically lived out in the terrifying realities of National Socialism and the Third Reich in Germany, and also in the consequences on human values of the Second World War. He called this accumulation of the results of the denial of God by a society founded on the belief in God as "retro-barbarism." It was a return to a fearsome, dehumanizing betrayal of everything this society had honored, appreciated, and celebrated.

These insights began to be articulated by Tsirindanes and his fellow Christian professional men and women in the mid-1940's. Over forty years later, the assessment has come to apply to America quite vividly. From this perspective, it is clear why even someone like Ronald Reagan could declare that the Leninist, atheistic Union of Soviet Socialist Republics is no longer an "evil empire" in the eyes of the Constitution-based capitalist United States of America. It may be that both the modern-day U.S.S.R. and the modern-day U.S.A. have more in common than we have otherwise thought: both share fully today in what Alexander Tsirindanes called negation and retro-barbarism.

4. Beyond criticism, beyond analysis. Professor Packer ends his paper with an appeal to this society "to return to the time-honored moral standards," to use his phrase. With a quote from the prophet Jeremiah (6:16-19), he also clearly does not expect the society to do this. By his use of the Jeremiah quote he indicates his expectation that this will bring "disaster on this people." And he ends with a prayer to God that this consequence may "not be irrevocably so in modern North America."

If this is a moral universe, and I believe to the core of my being that it is, his pessimistic assessment is probably accurate. The wages of sin are death, and I believe that our society these days is experiencing some symptoms of potential terminal illness. The whole litany of behaviors adopted by Western society seem to me to represent a decadent and dying society. In the sphere of ethics, scholars, teachers, yes, in many cases, even preachers have ceased the effort to determine the good and the right and the genuinely fitting and appropriate kinds of behaviors which human beings ought to follow. Rather, we see a genuine breakdown of our social structures, personal character and integrity, communities of meaning, and even our ecclesial convictions.

Nevertheless, regardless of what comes, believers in Jesus Christ cannot simply sit back and let events take their course. We are bearers of a cross, to be sure. But we are also committed to a message of good news for all the world. We have an "evangelical ethic," that is, a way of life rooted in the good news of the salvation of humanity and the whole created world, brought about by the life and work and mission of Jesus Christ and realized in history by the presence, energy, and activity of the Holy Spirit. And whether we want to accept it or not, the vehicle for this work is the church.

Alexander Tsirindanes, over forty years ago, was also not content with criticism and analysis. He called Christians to assume their real role as a leaven in society. Even in the face of the powerful forces of negation and the evident consequences of retro-barbarism, he called for a Christianity which was alive, that is, which realized in some measure the full range of God-like living. He called for a Christianity which was contemporary in its concern for people's lives and the human condition. He called for a Christianity which saw itself as having a guiding role for human beings and human society. He had a vision of the demand of the age for a Christianity which brought to the world the transfiguring power of God. Beyond the motto of "Living, Contemporized, Guiding, and Transforming Christianity," which Tsirindanes called for, is the reality of a fallen world, but also a world which still has hope as long as it is true that God still loves that world. I believe that is true. God still loves his fallen, disobedient, disoriented, confused, and sinful world. If God does, we who are called to serve him can do no less. In the last analysis, as the gospel says, our God is "not a God of the dead, but of the living; for all live to him" (Lk 20:38). Christians may never accede to the death of this civilization. We can never end with death as our vision. Ours is, finally and in the last analysis, a faith in a living God, one who has conquered death, and sin, and evil, and the demonic forces of life through his resurrection. Because Christ is risen, we can never give up!

SIX

A Roman Catholic Response to J.I. Packer

William E. May

PROFESSOR PACKER has beautifully summarized the fundamental structure of Christian morality and has outlined the major factors in modernist thinking that have sent it off course. My remarks will, I hope, complement elements of Professor Packer's analysis, in particular his emphasis on the relationship between orthodoxy or sound doctrine and orthopraxy or sound morality and on the question of anthropology. I will focus on the question of human dignity, contrasting the way in which this is differently conceived by the Christian tradition and by much modernist thought. In my conclusion I hope to show in a very concrete way how these differences shape our understanding of human existence.

According to the Christian tradition there is a twofold dignity proper to human beings: the first is intrinsic and is a pure gift or endowment; the second is also intrinsic, but it is an achievement made possible by the exercise of human freedom with the help of God's unfailing grace. I will consider each of these two forms of human dignity in turn, first presenting the Christian understanding and then contrasting it to the view entertained by much modernist thinking.

The first type of dignity attributed to human beings by the

Christian tradition is the dignity that is theirs simply as members of the human species, which God called into existence when, in the beginning, he "created man in his own image . . . male and female he created them" (Gn 1:27). Every living human body, the one that comes to be when new human life is conceived, is a living image of the all-holy God. In creating Man, male and female, God created a being inwardly receptive of his own inner divine life. God cannot become incarnate in a dog or pig or ape because these creatures of his are not inwardly capable of being divinized. But, as we know from God's revelation, he can become incarnate in his human creature, and in fact he has freely chosen to become one of us, for his eternal and uncreated Word, true God of true God, became and *is* a human being, a man. Thus every human being can rightly be said to be a "created word" of the Father, the created word that his uncreated Word became and is, precisely to show us how deeply we are loved by the God who formed us in our mothers' wombs (see Psalm 139:11-15). Every human being is, in short, a *person* made in the image and likeness of the God who is a trinity of persons.

Moreover, in creating man, male and female, God did not create a "conscious subject" to which he then, as an afterthought, added a body. Rather, in creating man he created a being of living flesh into which he breathed the "breath of life" (Gn 2:7). Human persons, therefore, are "body" persons; the human body is integral to the human person. So long, consequently, as we have in our midst a living human body, we have present among us a human person, a being of incalculable worth. Not all of these persons have the *developed* capacity for making true judgments and moral choices, but all, by virtue of being the kind of beings they are, have within themselves the capacity for knowing the truth and making free choices. All human beings are, by *being* human to begin with, radically different in kind from nonhuman animals, and of every living human body we can say, "Here is a person, not a thing. Here is a being made in God's image and likeness and inwardly capable of being divinized."

Precisely because human persons are "body" persons, Christian thought has always taken seriously the differences between males and females. Males and females, men and women, boys and girls, boy babies and girl babies, born or unborn, are indeed equally persons, equal in their dignity as living images of the all-holy God. Yet they differ in their sexuality, and their sexuality is more than skin deep, more than anatomical and physiological. For their bodily differences are revelatory of differences in the depths of their being as human beings. They are equal but differing and complementary epiphanies or manifestations or images of God, and their differences are of importance and need to be taken into account in structuring human society so that it can prosper as God wills.

Human sexuality, moreover, including its procreative aspect or its power to generate human life, is something that far surpasses the sexuality of the beasts. The generation of human life, therefore, is not an act of "reproduction," that is, of the mere multiplication of a biological species; it is an act of "procreation," of giving life to a new human person, and human persons, like the uncreated Word whose image they are, are to be "begotten" in an act of self-giving love, for they are beings equal in nature and in dignity to their progenitors, not objects to be "made" and inferior in nature to their producers.

The modernist view of human beings and of human personhood is quite different. To the modernist what is most important is consciousness and conscious experience. The body, as such, is, something that human beings share with the beasts. It is part of the physical world over which man, that is, the conscious subject, has dominion. Here the views of Joseph Fletcher, to whom Professor Packer referred in his paper, are typical of the modernist conception. According to Fletcher, "physical nature—the body and its members, our organs and their functions—all of these *things* are a part of 'what is over against us.' . . . Freedom, knowledge, choice, responsibility—all these things of personal or moral stature are in us, not *out there*. Physical nature is what is over against us, out there. It represents the world of *its*" (*Morals and Medicine* [Boston: Beacon Press, 1960], p. 221). The human body, in other words, is not, for the modernist, a good *of* the person, integral to the person. Rather it is a good *for* the person, something to be used by the person as he or she sees fit. The person, on the other hand, is the conscious subject aware of itself as a self and capable of relating to other selves.

On this modernist view, it follows that not all living human bodies are persons. Modernist thought makes a sharp distinction between being a member of the human species and being a person. Only those members of the human species who are actually capable of self-consciousness and of relating "meaningfully" to other conscious subjects are, in modernist thought, persons. Thus babies, newborn and preborn, are *not*, in this view, persons. Rather they are "things," subpersonal in nature and subject to the domination and manipulation of "conscious subjects." So too, in this view, are the seriously retarded and the senile, "vegetables" whose personality, so it is said, has been extinguished. Indeed, in modernist thought dolphins, chimpanzees, and even rats are closer to being "persons" than are unborn and newborn babies, Down's Syndrome children, or victims of Alzheimer's disease.

This modernist view, which prizes consciousness and conscious experience, is in many ways similar in character to the ancient gnosticism that was, in New Testament times, the most serious threat to Christianity. Like the gnostics of old, for instance, modernists disdain the flesh and regard with contempt life-long fidelity in a monogamous marriage committed to the procreation and education of children. In the modernist, as in the gnostic, scheme, sexual relations are valued not because of their connection to the generation of human life—for this, after all, is a beastly matter—but rather because of the conscious experiences such relations, whether heterosexual or homosexual, make possible. On this view, too, males and females are at bottom "persons," that is, conscious subjects aware of themselves as selves and capable of relating to other selves. Their differences are of no major importance, for their differences are merely biological, anatomical, physiological, not personal. As persons, they are not only equal but equivalent, with no meaningful differences between them.

The second kind of dignity that the Christian tradition attributes to human beings is the dignity that they are called upon to give to themselves by making free choices in accordance with the truth. Christian faith professes that God has given to man the gift of free, self-determining choice. According to Christian faith, human actions are not mere physical events that come and go, like the falling of the leaves. For at the core of a human action is a free, self-determining choice, whereby human persons give to themselves their moral identity, their character as persons who are morally good or morally bad. Through our choices we settle things in our "hearts" and give to ourselves a disposition to make further choices of the same kind. And our hearts, we know, must be clean and pure, open to what is good and true and beautiful. As our Lord teaches us, "There is no sound tree that produces rotten fruit, nor again a rotten tree that produces good fruit. For every tree can be told by its own fruit.... A good man draws what is good from the store of goodness in his heart; a bad man draws what is bad from the store of badness in his heart" (Lk 6:43-45).

It is thus most important that human persons make good choices. But how are we to know, prior to choice, which alternatives are good and which are bad? According to Christian faith "the highest norm of human life is the divine law, eternal, objective, and universal, whereby God orders, governs, and directs the entire universe according to a plan conceived in wisdom and in love" (Vatican Council II, *Dignitatis Humanae*, section 3). And God has so made man that he is able, under the gentle disposition of divine providence, to come to a knowledge of this law and its unchanging truths. "For man has in his heart a law written by God," and "*his dignity lies in observing this law*" (Vatican Council II, *Gaudium et Spes*, 16). Professor Packer has already well summarized this matter. What is most instructive in his remarks, I think, is the following: "What God commands is that we observe his prior determinations of what is good and bad, that is, his teaching about the kinds of actions that he loves and hates to see *and that make for or against the fulfillment of our created human nature*."

In order for human beings *to be* fully the beings God wills them to be, they must choose rightly, that is, in accordance with the truth. Moral norms, in other words, are by no means arbitrary and legalistic impositions inhibiting human fulfillment and happiness. Rather, they are liberating truths, rooted in God's wise and loving plan for human existence and inscribed by God into our very being, that enable us to choose well and rightly. They are the laws of our being, and only by choosing in accordance with them can we be true to our dignity as beings made in the image and likeness of God and summoned, through and in Christ, to be the very children of God, members of his divine family. As beings made in God's image we fulfill our being, carry out our vocation, and achieve the dignity to which we are called by making good moral choices in accordance with the truth.

All this takes on even added significance in the light of Christian faith. For the Christian knows that, in our human endeavor to be fully the beings we are meant to be, we can be crippled and we can be helped. We are crippled by sin; and, as a result of Adam's sin and our own sinful choices, we find ourselves powerless to do the good that we know (for example, see Romans 8). But God is our greatest and best friend, our enabler and helper. He has come, in the person of his only-begotten Son made man, "become flesh" (*sarx egeneto*, John 1:14) to redeem us from sin and to enable us, now dead to sin and risen to a new kind of life through our participation in Christ's saving deed, to be fully the beings God wills us to be. Our glorious task is to participate in Christ's redemptive work, to overcome evil with good, to love, even as we have been and are loved by God in Christ.

God's law, moreover, includes moral norms that are absolute in character, unchanging and indefeasible. There are certain sorts or kinds of human choices and actions that are utterly incompatible with God's love and completely opposed to his wise and loving plan for human existence. Professor Packer has noted all this in his magnificent address. Adultery, fornication, envy, the killing of the innocent—actions of these and similar kinds are absolutely and completely opposed to God's law. Those who choose to be, through their actions, adulterers, fornicators, killers, etc., make themselves to be evildoers, persons whose hearts are closed to the goods of human existence and to the source whence these goods spring, the all-holy and triune God.

On the modernist view there are no moral absolutes (although, as we shall see, there is *one* that modernists like Joseph Fletcher proclaim). There are no absolutes because for them there is no unchanging law of God. Valuing conscious experience as they do, they propose that in making choices we choose that alternative that will bring about the greater proportion of good over evil. This proposal, as Professor Packer has shown, is simply unworkable. But for the modernist it makes some sense, for to the modernist mind the good is what is consciously experienced as such. So all they do is state their preferences before making their choices and then rationalize their choices in terms of their self-chosen goals. Prizing, as they do, self-conscious experiences and the values of control over their lives and the liberty to do as they see fit, they can always justify the "creative" act of adultery or of sodomy or the "liberating" act of killing the innocent.

Yet there is one absolute in the modernist vision of things, namely, the absolute that "no unwanted baby ought ever to be born," an absolute championed by Joseph Fletcher and a host of contemporaries. In the name of this absolute they proclaim the liberty of all to contracept and abort, and, should an unwanted baby slip by these nets, to kill the newborn who suffers from the tort of "wrongful life." This absolute, I believe, is the hallmark of modernism and of the contemporary mind. It has subtly worked its way into the thought of many modern Christian theologians, Catholic and Protestant, and has, unfortunately, in many ways become public policy in our nation, where an unwanted pregnancy is now regarded as a form of venereal disease, one to be "cured" by the therapy of abortion.

In contrast to this slogan typical of the modernist approach to morality, which has severed the bonds uniting the life-giving meanings of human sexuality and speaks instead of "baby making" and "love making" as two separate sorts of human endeavor, stands the truth of the gospel: "No person ought ever to be unwanted." And the only way to build a society in which all persons are wanted is to develop a society in which men and women freely choose to shape their lives in accordance with God's law, where they choose to be chaste and to respect every living human body as an irreplaceable and nonsubstitutable person, refusing to regard the human body as an object of enjoyment or of use.

Part II

Facing the Challenges

SEVEN

The Christian View of Sex: A Time for Apologetics, Not Apologies

Janet E. Smith

I T IS NOT A NOVEL INSIGHT to observe that we live in a society that is suffering greatly from sexual confusion or, if you will, sexual misconduct. There is little need here to provide a full set of statistics to demonstrate the consequences of the sexual revolution, for who is not familiar with the epidemic in teenage pregnancies, venereal diseases, AIDS, and the rest? Our society has been undergoing a rapid transformation in terms of sexual behavior, and few of us would argue that it is for the better. For instance, only ten years ago there was one divorce for every three marriages; now there is one for every two marriages. The millions of abortions over the last decade alone indicate that our society has serious problems with sexuality. Ten years ago the statistics of sexual disorder were bad enough; many thought things could hardly get worse—as did many twenty years ago, and thirty years ago. In the last generation the incidence of sexual activity outside of marriage, with all the accompanying problems, has doubled and tripled—or worse. We have no particular reason to believe that we have seen the peak of the growth in sexually related problems.

Statistics do not capture the pervasive ills attendant upon sexual immorality. Premature and promiscuous sexuality prevent many from establishing good marriages and a good family life. Few deny that a healthy sexuality and a strong family life are among the most necessary elements for human happiness and well-being. It is well attested that strong and secure families are more likely to produce strong and secure individuals, individuals less likely to have problems with alcohol, sex, and drugs, individuals more likely to be free from crippling neuroses and psychoses. Since healthy individuals are not preoccupied with their own problems, they are able to be strong leaders; they are prepared to tackle the problems of society. While many single parents do a worthy and valiant job of raising their children, it remains sadly true that children from broken homes grow up to be adults with a greater propensity for crime, a greater tendency to engage in alcohol and drug abuse, and a greater susceptibility to psychological disorders.

These realities affect every realm of life—they affect people's ability to relate to friends and family; they affect the whole of society which needs stable and secure individuals to lead us out of our troubles. And those who do not experience love from family and friends tend to seek any semblance of love they can find—and thus become involved in illicit sexual relationships—and the cycle starts again. The multiple varieties of abuse of sexuality and the grievous consequences of such abuse, then, are not only damaging the current generation, but are threatening to ruin the chances of future generations to live happy and fulfilled lives.

Twenty years ago when the sexual revolution was beginning to be in full swing, many argued that the value of the sexual revolution was that it was going to liberate men and women from the repressive view of sexuality pervasive in society. People would be free to make love to those whom they loved without the strictures of marriage. Many pointed to Christianity as the source of sexual repression. But the Christian view of sex, once considered a distorted view of sexuality, is now beginning to look a lot more like wisdom. Christians no longer need to offer apologies for their insistence upon sexual morality, for their insistence upon reserving sex for marriage. Some in high public places are now beginning to counsel abstinence before marriage and to extol faithful monogamous marriage. They have begun to see these as practices of great practical wisdom. Christians, of course, have long recognized the practical value of chastity and fidelity, but have also recognized them as practices in accord with God's will for mankind.

In a certain sense, Christian morality—especially in regard to sexual morality—is quite similar to natural morality or common sense morality. One does not need to be a Christian to understand why certain sexual practices are wrong. Christians differ from unbelievers not so much in the understanding of what is moral and immoral as in their commitment to trying to do what is moral. Christians understand that when they are doing wrong they are not only violating good sense, they are violating God's law; they are failing to be the loving and responsible persons God made them to be. Thus, Christian apologetics about sex may not seem much different from common sense apologetics about sex, but it is the Christian tradition which has most faithfully preserved the common wisdom about sex. Clearly it is easy to forget or become confused about the common wisdom about sex. Christians are blessed with the powerful aid of revelation and tradition to keep them straight on what constitutes sexual morality.

Yet, although most Christian denominations have remained steadfast in their allegiance to traditional Christian wisdom in sexual issues, few Christians have not been deeply affected by the saturation of our modern cultural forms with a view of sexuality radically opposed to the Christian view. Ten minutes of watching MTV or a soap opera, ten minutes of listening to any rock, pop, or country-Western music station, one visit to the corner store magazine rack, or two minutes at the beach should serve to convince the most skeptical that our society has very little respect for the Christian moral norms regarding sexual relations. Christians, too, have begun to lose sight of the understanding of sexuality advanced by their tradition. Thus, now is the time for Christians to offer apologetics for their understanding of the role of sexual relations within human relationships.

"Apologetics" is a term used to refer to the energetic attempt to explain one's position to others. But Christians, I think, need to be as concerned with providing apologetics or explanations to themselves about sex as they need to bring their message to others. Both internal and external evangelizing are necessary, for few, if any can escape being adversely affected by the distortions of our times. Christians need to strengthen themselves. Christians have much to learn about their own tradition before they can become effective witnesses to those in the larger society who desperately need to encounter individuals in control of their sexuality and happy because of it.

There are a multitude of Christian truths which bear upon sexuality and which would assist Christians and others in escaping the ravages of a disordered sexuality. The time seems to be ripe for making the most persuasive case we can for Christian morality. Certainly, some are ceasing to pursue promiscuous relationships because of their fear of contracting AIDS. But this is not the only reason for the growing disenchantment with the sexual revolution. Many find themselves lonely after their sexual encounters and are looking for something more. There are increasing reports of sexual indifference; many claim to have lost an interest in sex, even with those whom they love. And, while many may not have moral objections to premarital sex and abortion, there seems to be an increasing weariness with these phenomena and an increasing interest in reducing both. Many are beginning to see that the call for more and better sex education, or more and better access to contraceptives, is not the solution. Rather, we need a better understanding of the relation of sex, love, marriage, and children. And it is this understanding that I think Christianity can provide.

Here let us focus on three fundamental truths about sexuality stressed throughout the Christian tradition: (1) marriage is the proper arena for sexual activity; (2) marriages must be faithful for the love of spouses to thrive; and (3) children are a great gift to spouses. Christian teaching about sexuality also provides guidelines for those with homosexual leanings, and for discerning the morality of a whole host of sexual practices. Here I shall focus primarily upon the Christian understanding of marriage, for if we grasp the basics of this understanding, the implications for most other kinds of sexual activity are fairly clear.

Marriage the Place for Sexual Union

Those attempting to provide apologetics or explanations should have a sense of the needs and views of their audience. As has been suggested above, it is safe to assume that modern Americans have a casual notion of sex. They think it is natural for those who love one another to engage in sexual union, whether married or not, and often whether of the same sex or not. But most have begun to see that happiness is rarely achieved through promiscuity. They have begun to acknowledge that premarital sex has done little to ensure good marriages; they fear that teenage sex and abortions may cause lifetime scars on young people's psyches. To these people we must make the case that happiness, true intimacy, and sexual fulfillment are more naturally found within faithful marriages.

What are the reasons for saying that it is appropriate for sexual union to take place only within marriage? It is hardly deniable that sexual union creates powerful bonds between individuals, even often among those who do not desire such bonds. Those who have sexual intercourse with each other are engaging in an action which bespeaks a deep commitment to the other. The current Pope uses an interesting phrase in his teachings on sex, and that is the term "language of the body," which is not so very different from our "body language." He claims bodily actions have meanings much as words do and that unless we intend those meanings with our actions we should not perform them, any more than we should speak words we do not mean. In both cases, lies are being "spoken." Sexual union has a well-recognized meaning; it means "I find you attractive," "I care for you," "I will try to work for your happiness," "I wish to have a deep bond with you." Some who engage in sexual intercourse do not mean these things with their actions; they wish simply to use another for their own sexual pleasure. They have lied with their bodies in the same way as someone lies who says, "I love you," to another simply for the purposes of obtaining some desired favor.

But some engaging in sexual intercourse outside of marriage claim that they mean all that sexual union means and that therefore they are not lying with their bodies. They are, though, making false promises, for those engaging in sexual intercourse outside of marriage cannot fulfill the promises their bodily actions make. They have not prepared themselves to fulfill the promise of working for another's happiness or achieving a deep bond with another. For such achievements take a lifetime to complete; they cannot be accomplished in brief encounters.

The existence of the institution of marriage acknowledges the importance of love for the happiness of human beings, the importance of the lifetime unconditional love that marriage facilitates. Humans flourish when they bask in the love of others. Love nourishes human goodness like no other force. For instance, love assists us in feeling secure in ourselves; it gives us the confidence to dare to exercise our talents; it gives us the assurance to reach out to others in love. Love also serves to heal past wounds. Love in almost any form can promote these and other great benefits to mankind, but marital love provides special benefits. Human beings are com- plicated, are not easily known by themselves or others; a lifetime relationship with another seems hardly time enough to get to know another. Sexual intimacy plays a major role in the revealing of one person to another. Sexual intimacy provides an opportunity for giving oneself to another in an exclusive way. Only in marriage can sexual intimacy achieve the goals it is meant to serve.

The Christian insistence on reserving sexual union for marriage, then, has as one of its chief justifications a concern that sexual union is meant to express the desire for a deep and committed relationship with another. That relationship can only be built within marriage, for marriage is built upon a vow of faithfulness to one's beloved. The Bible, especially the Old Testament, regularly condemns the sin of adultery. Faithful marriage is used regularly as the paradigm for the kind of relationship which God's people should have with God. Those who are not faithful to God are likened to adulterers. The Book of Proverbs and the rest of the biblical wisdom literature harshly condemns the adulterous spouse. Most spouses are devas- tated at the mere thought that their beloved desired another, let alone that their spouse may have actually been unfaithful. Faithfulness is essential to create the relationship of trust which is the bedrock of all the other goods that flow from marriage.

We take vows in marriage because we realize that we are all too ready to give up when the going gets tough; we realize that our loves wax and wane. Indeed, society at large seems to have a fondness for marriage. After all, in an age where there is little moral pressure against living together outside of marriage, most still choose to take marriage vows. Couples realize that marriage vows help them express and effect the commitment they feel for each other. But as the divorce rate indicates, modern society ultimately does not take these vows very seriously—or at least modern couples do not prepare for marriage in such a way that they are prepared to keep their vows.

Let me speak for a moment about marriage preparation. I am not speaking here of the engagement encounter weekend, the talk with the pastor, or the pre-Cana conference in which engaged couples participate. I am speaking about the kind of preparation which we must do for ourselves for many years before we enter marriage. Many young people enjoy the exercise of drawing up a list of characteristics they would like their future spouse to have. But their time would be better spent drawing up a list of characteristics which they themselves should have in order to be a worthy marriage partner. They need, too, to reflect upon their expectations of marriage; many may come to see that their expectations are largely selfish. Most of us dream much more about how happy our spouses are going to make us rather than about how much we are going to do for our spouses.

Since marriage requires loving, faithful, kind, patient, forgiving, humble, courageous, wise, unselfish individuals—and the list could go on—young people should strive to gain these characteristics. Marriage cannot survive unless the spouses acquire these characteristics. Certainly it would be foolish to require that individuals have all these characteristics before they marry, for none of us do. Indeed, the experience of marriage itself undoubtedly helps foster these characteristics. But the fact is that if we do not work at acquiring these characteristics before marriage, we will be acquiring their opposites, such as selfishness, and haughtiness, and impatience—characteristics that are death to a marriage.

For many it seems odd to speak of the need to be faithful to one's spouse before marriage, but such is the case. In a sense, one should love one's spouse before one even meets him or her. One should be preparing to be a good lover, a good spouse, one's whole life. This means reserving the giving of one's self sexually until one is married—for in a sense, one's sexuality belongs to one's future spouse as much as it does to one's self. A few generations ago, it was not uncommon for young people to speak of "saving themselves" for marriage. It is a phrase scoffed at today, but nonetheless indicative of a proper understanding of love, sexuality, and marriage. One should prepare one's self for marriage and one should save one's self for marriage.

How does one do so? Obviously by remaining chaste—and that is not an easy prescription. For instance, it means being attentive to what provokes sexual thoughts and desires and avoiding these provocations. It means, most likely, dissociating one's self from many of the forms of entertainment popular today. Those who have a view of sexuality as a gift which one offers one's spouse at the time of marriage cannot afford to be victim to the constant sexual stimulation modern Americans face daily. So we need to be careful what music we listen to, what movies and TV shows we watch, and we need to try to dress modestly. We need to try to save sexual thoughts and sexual stimulation for the time when they will not be frustrations but will be welcome preludes to loving union with our spouse. Sexual temptations are, of course, impossible to avoid, especially since our society does not seek to make it easier for us; rather it provides temptations around the clock. Christ's teaching that lust in one's heart is wrong tells us that we must guard our inner purity as well as govern our actions.

It must be acknowledged that few think it sensible for those who are engaged to wait until their wedding night to enjoy sexual union. This view seems to be nearly as widespread among Christians as in the rest of society. Many think waiting until marriage would make sexual intimacy too awkward; that it is good to have a more relaxed and casual time to get to know one another sexually. Most think that since one is soon going to take vows, it makes little difference whether sexual intimacy begins before or after a ceremony which simply ratifies a commitment already felt.

What difference does waiting make? Well, certainly a vow is not a vow until it is spoken; unspoken, unratified commitments are all too easily broken. But there are practical reasons as well. Father James Burtchaell at the University of Notre Dame, has written a marvelous book, For Better or Worse, laying out many of the reasons why it is best for couples to wait until marriage before they begin their sexual intimacy. He speaks eloquently of the period before marriage as an irreplaceable opportunity for the lovers to get to know one another. Engaging in sexual intercourse creates a false sense of closeness. It creates a bond that may obscure elements in a relationship which need to be worked on. Courtship is a privileged time for talking and getting to know each other; for sketching out dreams and plans; for expressing worries and hesitations. The delight of sexual union can easily be a disincentive to working out all the matters that those who are getting married should work out.

But there is perhaps a deeper reason, and that is the question of honesty and trust. Few of those having sexual relations before marriage, especially Christians, can be fully open about their actions.

This means that individuals engaging in such relationships must inevitably be deceiving someone—most likely their parents, their teachers, and perhaps their friends as well. The ability to practice such deception does not bode well for one's integrity. The lovers observe that each is good at deceiving. They will file away this information and will most likely have reason to wonder in the future if the other is being honest. After all, one's beloved had no trouble deceiving others whom he or she respected. Many Christians feel terrible guilt at violating their own deeply held moral principles. Some after they are married tend to have guilty feelings about sex. In a sense, they have programmed themselves to think of sexual intercourse as a furtive and naughty activity.

Couples who do wait until marriage to enjoy sexual union often seem to have a special kind of euphoria about their sexual union. Because they have waited, they feel entitled to sexual enjoyment and see it as a privileged good of marriage. They have an easier time developing a deep and abiding trust and consideration for each other. Their willingness to wait, their willingness to endure the strains of sexual continence because they love and respect one another, is a great testimony to their strength of character. They have also shown that sexual attraction is not the most important part of the relationship. They have shown that they enjoy each other's company even when the delights of sexual union are not available to them. Such faithfulness and chastity before marriage insure greater faithfulness and chastity during marriage, when, because of pregnancy or illness or separation, all couples must abstain at some time. The acquisition of the virtue of self-mastery before marriage facilitates such necessary abstention.

Sex and Childbearing

Young people need to be chaste before marriage not only because of the love they hope to share with their future spouses, but also because of the responsibilities they have to their future children. Years ago the chief reason for refraining from sexual activity before marriage was fear of pregnancy. Pregnancy was feared both because young people were not prepared to take care of their children and also because there was considerable societal disapproval of sexual intercourse before marriage. The societal disapproval is gone, and contraceptives have largely removed the fear—though not the reality—of unwanted pregnancies. Indeed, contraception seems to be one of the chief facilitators of much of the sexual misconduct of our times. There certainly were many fewer teenage pregnancies, many fewer abortions, a lesser incidence of sexually transmitted diseases, and so on, before contraception became widely available. Contraception has made people feel secure that they can have sexual union apart from the obligations of marriage and child-rearing. Yet contraceptives do not remove the responsibilities that come with the child-making possibilities of sexual intercourse. Young people are notoriously irresponsible about nearly everything. They are roughly as responsible about using contraceptives as they are about doing their homework, hanging up their clothes, and doing their chores. And even those who use contraceptives are not really safe, since contraceptives do not always work. We must drive home to our young people that they are not ready for sexual intercourse until they are ready to be parents, for sexual intercourse always brings with it the possibility of being a parent.

Getting young people to associate sex with childbearing is not easy, but it is necessary. In fact, it is important for adults to encourage young people to try to think like a parent. It is wise for parents to talk about parenting with their children. It is good to get them thinking about what they would like to do with their children; to get them thinking about what they want to be able to provide for their children. And parents must convey to their children that they are not a burden to them, that they consider their children to be great gifts from God. Our society almost universally looks upon children as a burden; they are expensive, noisy, troublesome; they stand in the way of careers and adventuresome travel. This view, of course, has not stopped people from having babies, but one senses that many children are just another possession of their parents or just another experience that adults wish to have. Many couples seem to want to have a few "designer children" as ornaments to their lives—not as reasons for their lives.

God, it seems, has a preference for children. After all, one of his first commands was "be fruitful and multiply." Throughout the Old Testament, having many children is listed among the signs of prosperity that indicate God's favor. Psalm 127 states, "Behold, sons are a gift from the Lord; the fruit of the womb is a reward. Like arrows in the hand of a warrior are the sons of one's youth. Happy the man whose quiver is filled with them." Psalm 128 is one of my favorites; it states:

> For you shall eat the fruit of your handiwork; happy shall you be, and favored.
> Your wife shall be like a fruitful vine in the recesses of your home;
> Your children like olive plants around your table.
> Behold, thus is the man blessed who fears the Lord.

God has arranged matters so that parents and children need each other. The experience of parenting, like the experience of marriage, both requires and fosters many virtues. Having children generally does adults a lot of good. Most find themselves becoming more selfless, more patient, kind, loving, and tender, when they have children. Learning to live with children has many of the same advantages of living with a spouse. It forces one to accommodate one's self to others, to acknowledge that one has constant tendencies to be selfish. Staying awake at night with children, dealing with their daily joys and sorrows, learning to be a good example for them contribute greatly to the maturity of adults.

Christians have a radically different view of children from the rest of society. They understand that their offspring are not possessions through which they can live their unfulfilled dreams and have another way of winning the respect of the world around them. Rather, Christians see children as a gift of God, as souls entrusted to them, whom they are to return to God. Among Christians there is a predisposition towards children, for Christians understand that God loves life and wishes to share his glorious creation. Christians are generally more eager and willing to have children because they realize the importance of children to God and depend on him to assist them in providing for the children he has given them.

Recently a relative of mine mentioned that he wanted to have a large family but that he did not know how it would be possible to manage financially. He had noticed that I had a large number of friends who started their childbearing early and had lots of children. Few of the women have paying jobs. He wanted to know how they did it. The question is a good one, and I think I know the answer: they trust in God. They regularly live on the edge of things—for the first few years they experience occasional anxiety that another child will be undue strain on the budget, or they fear that they will not be able to afford a car or house large enough for the growing brood, or they fear that they may not be able to meet food and medical costs. But after a few years, they find that in most surprising and often in quite spectacular ways, their needs are fulfilled. To be sure, they learn to budget and scrimp and save, and they are not ashamed to take hand-me-downs, and they often learn to live a life that is a little tacky around the edges. But they lack none of their true needs and often enjoy luxuries they never would have dreamed of having. So they come to trust God and live without a lot of obvious security. Trust in God replaces the American desire for perfect security. They do not set their sights on accumulating enough money and material goods to serve as a buffer against the world. With trusting hearts and light hearts they proceed to enjoy their growing families and to soak up the love that flows in big families. And they become ever more generous with what they have. Those with large families seem to have a special generosity and hospitality about them. Guests are extremely welcome and interruptions seem not to be the annoyance they are for most; members of large families seem quite ready to drop everything to help someone else. Slowly but steadily they become better Christians.

Contraception and Generous Childbearing

Here I would like to broach a topic which is sensitive and controversial; it is a topic about which I have been doing much research; and that is the topic of contraception. I am now doing revisions on the manuscript for a book on *Humanae Vitae*, the encyclical written by Pope Paul VI which taught that the use of contraceptives is immoral. The teaching has been nearly completely discounted by society as a whole and widely ignored by Catholics as well. Nonetheless, I have found a wisdom in this teaching which I would like to promote among both my Catholic and non-Catholic sisters and brothers in the Lord. One of the great fruits of ecumenism, of course, is that different traditions can learn much from each other. But it is wrong to think that opposition to contraception is a distinctively Catholic doctrine. It surprises many to learn that the belief that contraception is not in accord with God's will is not a distinctive Catholic belief. The fact is that all Protestant denominations were also opposed to contraception up until 1930. The Anglican Church twice early in this century condemned contraception and then for the first time in 1930 passed a resolution that it was morally permissible for spouses to use contraception. Thus, in the Christian scheme of things, acceptance of contraception is a relatively new phenomenon. Catholics have, perhaps, preserved the teaching against contraception more faithfully, but it has not been a teaching exclusive to them.

In much the same way Protestants have more faithfully preached the necessity of tithing, a doctrine not exclusive to Protestants. Many Catholics are now rediscovering the practice of tithing—many of them at the prompting of their Protestant brethren. They have found great spiritual growth through this practice and now in the Catholic press regularly urge their fellow Catholics to embrace this time-honored way of being grateful to God and of trusting in him. Indeed, I think the doctrine on tithing has some similarities with the teaching that in one's childbearing one must be generous with God. Some refuse to tithe since they think it foolish to give away money that they think they need for their own well-being. Yet, those who are committed to tithing know that on occasion one must give to God what one believes one needs one's self. They give to God and his causes because they know he wants them to, and they trust him to provide. Being generous in childbearing is not so very different. Many a married couple will testify to their belief that they thought having another child would be an undue hardship, only to find that having another child was a source of wonderful blessing and splendid joy to them.

Of course, few would deny that couples on occasion may have good reason to curtail their childbearing at least for a while. Few argue that sometimes spouses would be more responsible in not having more children at a certain time than in having children. This being the case, many do not see why couples may not responsibly use contraceptives to help them space their children or delay child-bearing, if sufficiently good reason exists. They consider contraception a marvelous invention of technology, like many other forms of medicine, and see no reason not to use it, if used responsibly. They find the Catholic counsel of periodic abstinence to be rather irrational. They reason that both contraception and natural methods of family planning are designed to limit family size, so why not use the most effective method?

Oddly enough, natural family planning, or NFP, is one of the most effective means, if not the most effective means, of planning one's family. NFP, of course, is not the outmoded rhythm method, a method which was based on the calendar. Rather, NFP is a highly scientific way of determining when a woman is fertile based on observing various bodily signs. The statistics of its reliability rival the most effective forms of the Pill. And NFP is without the health risks and dubious moral status of contraceptives. It has long been known that the IUD is an abortifacient, that is, it works by causing an early-term abortion. Ovulation still occurs and therefore conception may occur; the IUD then prohibits the fertilized egg, the tiny new human being, from implanting in the wall of the uterus. Furthermore, the Pill and the IUD have proven to be dangerous to women in many ways. Currently the IUD is off the market in the United States because of the many lawsuits brought against its leading manufacturer. So those who are opposed to abortion and those interested in protecting the well-being of women would certainly not want to promote these forms of contraception. The other forms have aesthetic drawbacks or are low on reliability.

NFP no longer means "not for Protestants." Many non-Catholics are turning to NFP as a means of family planning precisely because they do not want to use abortifacients and they fear the physical risks of contraception. They are finding as a pleasant effect of their decision that the use of NFP has positive results for their marital relationship, for their relationship with their children, and for their relationship with God.

Many find it odd that periodic abstinence should be beneficial rather than harmful to marriage. Certainly most who begin to use NFP, especially those who were not chaste before marriage and who have used contraception, generally find the abstinence required to be a source of strain and a cause of considerable irritability. Abstinence, of course, like dieting or any form of self-restraint, brings its hardships. But like dieting and other forms of self-denial, it also brings its reward. As spouses learn to communicate better with each other—and abstinence gives them the opportunity to do so—as they learn to communicate their affection in nongenital ways, and as they learn to master their sexual desires, they find a new liberation in the ability to abstain from sexual intercourse. Many find that an element of romance reenters the relationship during the times of abstinence and an element of excitement accompanies the reuniting. Spouses using NFP find that they come to understand and respect one another more. Let me quote from a letter written by a woman who has used the whole gamut of contraceptive possibilities. Some of the language is rather crude, but it is not anything you don't hear nightly on TV—and during family viewing time, at that.

Though my hands are full with children (three) and with work outside the home (retail clerk), I feel moved to write in defense of the sexual sensibilities of those millions of us who are not PhDs or DREs [Directors of Religious Education] or [Phil] Donahue dissent superstars or even wanna-be's.

Yes, I was alive and fertile in 1968. I was 19 and I *knew* the Pill was a gift from God and *Humanae Vitae* was a real crock. The Pill was going to eliminate teenage pregnancy, marital disharmony, and world population problems, bring a new era, etc.

By my five-year reunion (high school) those of us who had been so confident about contraception had gone from euphoria to anger. Nothing seemed to work. I'd been on the Pill less that two years before I'd quit. The Pill depressed us. Or scared us (especially those of us who were smokers) because of the "stroke" factor. I didn't want to keep taking it year after year, or on-again off-again after I broke up with my college lover. So I decided to live a minimally healthy life style and quit both smoking and oral contraceptives.

The "safer" IUD (copper-T) gave me cramps and heavy periods. I was lucky. A friend of mine got such a ghastly infection from her IUD she lost her uterus, tubes, ovaries—the works. The woman was devastated. She felt like a gutted shell. Now they've taken them all off the market.

I tried the diaphragm. Hard to keep motivated on that one. . . . I felt wadded up with junk, inwardly disgusted. I wanted to be delectable, like a Haagen Dazs ice cream cone; instead, I was a spermicidal sump . . .

By the 10th high school reunion, my friends were still fiddling with this method and that, they'd had abortions, and/or their marriages were falling apart. Mine almost did.

Then my husband and I settled on condom plus periodic abstinence. But we depended on the condom in a way that made it easy to rationalize some "fudging" on abstinence. ("I'm probably fertile, but hey, we've got the ol' rubber so what harm can it do?") You know what "fudging" can lead to. Thank God I didn't have an abortion, but I did have one hell of an untimely pregnancy. Are you getting my point, fantasy-land theologians? Finally, my husband and I reached a turning point. At a very low point in our marriage, we met some great people who urged us to really give our lives to the Lord and to be chaste in our marriage.

That blew our minds. We thought it meant "give up sex." That's not what it means. It means respecting bodily union as a sacred act. It meant acting like a couple in love, a couple in *awe*, not a couple of cats in heat. For my husband and me, it meant NFP (natural family planning) with no rubber, no "fudging." And I won't kid you, it was a difficult discipleship.

NFP and a chaste attitude toward sex in marriage opened up a new world for us. It bonded my husband and me in a way that is so deep, so strong, that it's hard to describe. Sometimes it's difficult, but that makes us even closer. We revered each other. And when we do come together, we're like honeymooners.

Sad to say, I was past 35 when I finally realized that the church was right after all. Not the grab-your-sincerity-and-slide church of Charlie Curran, but the real church, the church we encountered through laypeople in the Couple to Couple League, the *Catholic* church. The church is right about contraception (it stinks), right about marriage (it's a sacrament), right about human happiness (it flows—no, it *floods* when you embrace the will of God). It gave us depth. It opened our hearts to love.

Put *that* in your graduate seminar and smoke it."

Roberta Roane
Brookville, Maryland

(*National Catholic Reporter,* October 11, 1986)

Why is it that couples who initially and perhaps constantly find difficult the restraint required by NFP, eventually come to sing the praises of NFP? One of the answers seems to be that couples advance in the virtue of self-mastery through their use of NFP. That is, they begin to realize that their sexual feelings can be controlled to some degree and that they need to be subordinated to the goods of marriage. Thus, if spouses determine that they could not responsibly have another child at a given time, they have the self-mastery to control their sexuality so that it does not conflict with what they have determined to be good for the family. This self-mastery that they gain spills over into their family life and the rest of their life with favorable results. Again, whenever we gain self-control, whether through curtailing our eating or drinking or spending, or in our sexual gratification—all activities good in themselves but in need of control—this self-control becomes somewhat easier in other realms of our lives.

Spouses using NFP become very good examples to their children, especially their teenagers, who may be wrestling with new and powerful sexual feelings. One man told me about how his practice of NFP assisted him in being a good witness for chastity among the young men at his place of work. They would tease him about being able, as a married man, to have sex on demand (it goes to show how much they know about marriage). But he responded that through the use of NFP he was required to abstain. He argued that if night after night he was able to sleep beside the woman he loved and not have sexual intercourse with her, they could learn to refrain from sexual intercourse with their girlfriends. He believed that parents who practice NFP could much more persuasively urge their children to be chaste before marriage.

Another reason given for the enthusiasm among couples for NFP is their view that couples who use NFP experience a greater bonding than those who use contraception. They claim that there is a more complete giving of one's self to another in a noncontracepted act of sexual intercourse than in a contracepted act. Certainly, no responsible person engages in noncontracepted sexual intercourse with one whom one does not want to have a significant bond—for noncontracepted intercourse brings with it the potential (sometimes symbolic) of having a child together, and children represent a lifetime bond. Those engaging in contracepted intercourse may intend a lifetime bond, but their actions do not express this intention. Those arguing this point cite as strong evidence for their position the claim that couples who practice NFP seem to have a nearly nonexistent divorce rate. Couples who use NFP also claim that it brings them closer to God. They believe that God made the human body and that respecting the way the human body works is a way of respecting God. They believe that contraceptives are an obstacle not only to union with their spouses but also to union with God. Couples not infrequently feel that God is present in a special way during their love-making. The emotions that flow and the bonding that takes place during love-making are of a grand and mysterious—not to say sacred—nature. They believe that God is the source of love and life and that he has privileged them with being the transmitters of life through an act of love. They feel that by not contracepting they are leaving God space to perform his act of the creation of a new soul, if he so chooses.

I hope this discussion has served to explain at least to some extent why for nearly the whole of its existence the Christian tradition has been opposed to the use of contraception. I did not go into some of the more complicated moral arguments, nor did I try to address likely objections. I simply wanted to link this teaching with the view that childbearing is an essential characteristic of marriage. Certainly it is undeniable that much of the Christian understanding of the need for faithful marriages and for the reserving of sexual intimacy for marriage is linked to the power of sexual union to result in children. Christians must work to convince themselves and others that we should never lose sight of the link between sexual activity and childbearing. If no one engaged in sexual union who was not prepared to care for any children who result from that union, the modern world would experience a radical change in its sexual behavior.

Christians need to provide apologetics and explanations why faithfulness and why responsibility towards children are two of the defining characteristics of marriage. Moderns, I think, are tired of unfaithfulness, tired of shallow and brief relationships. They crave something more meaningful, something on which they can rely. Young people are rather sick of divorce. There is virtually no one who does not know some children who have suffered greatly from divorce. Certainly many of us because of our own foolishness, weakness, or wickedness, or because of the foolishness, weakness, or wickedness of others, may not be able to form the marriages and families which we want and need. We must trust in the grace of God to provide for all those who turn to him for aid when matters are not as they ought to be. But the inability of many of us to live or to find what we know to be best is not a repudiation of what is best. Christians who have the wisdom of the centuries should themselves strive mightily to live chaste lives and to form loving marriages and families, for such is vital to their eternal salvation and such may well be vital to the temporal well-being of the whole society.

EIGHT

Christian Community Alternatives for Work, Culture, and Politics

John H. White

A SOCIETY IN PERIL desperately needs a people of God who will be the preserving salt and the redeeming light of that society in the areas of work, politics, and culture. Here I will argue that the biblical command requires that God's people be a distinctive alternative community in the world. Furthermore, I will offer some ecumenical examples of God's people acting in such a way and thus bringing a measure of amelioration to God's world.

We begin our study with the recognition that across the Christian spectrum we have had at least two reactions to the relationship of the gospel to the spheres of work, culture, and politics. One has been an attempt to make the gospel and Christian discipleship relevant to the life of the world by accommodation. To state it candidly, it has been a progressive attempt to rid the Christian message of its supernatural "baggage" so that it might speak to work, politics, and culture. Peter Berger put it like this: "Protestant theologians have been increasingly engaged in playing a game whose rules have been dictated by their 'cognitive antagonists.'"[1] In spite of a brief love affair with neo-orthodoxy, the recent theological novelties simply take up where the old Liberalism left off. To oversimplify it, it is the demise of the supernatural and the authority of God's revelation. Paul Tillich, whose influence cuts across Catholicism and Protestantism, understood the task of theology as a correlation and even syncretism between the Christian tradition and philosophical truth. Because of its marvelous authority structure, the Roman Catholic situation should have been different, but it was not. Into the early twentieth century there was an admirable holy defiance of what was called "progress, liberalism, and civilization as lately introduced."[2] In sharp contrast to that holy defiance, Hans Kung has written, "Churches today no longer want to be backward subcultures; organizations out of touch with the prevailing mentality. . . . The theologians want to leave traditional orthodoxy behind them and to make a serious attempt to bring scholarly integrity to bear on the dogmas and the Bible."[3]

Thus in both Roman Catholic and Protestant theology there is a pervasive tendency to relate the Christian faith to work, culture, politics by an accommodation that robs the faith of its heart.

On the other hand, the so-called Bible-believing evangelical community has had an endemic world-flight mentality. They are defenders of the faith once delivered to the saints. Yet that defensiveness has been fueled by a pietism that speaks of a personal relationship with Jesus which is both individualistic and intensely inward in its focus. The word "world" will almost always connote sin, anti-God. It seems to this writer something of the same thing has been true in Roman Catholic theology and Christian experience. Though the phrases are different from "a personal relationship with Christ," they are nevertheless similar because they speak of personal, inward, mystical, and usually sacramental experiences.

The Anglican writer Harry Blamires speaks to these two Bible-believing responses by Christians. He observes that the Christian

accepts religion, its morality, its worship, its spiritual culture; but he rejects the religious view of life, the view which sets all earthly issues within the context of the eternal, the view which relates all human problems—social, political, cultural—to the doctrinal foundations of the Christian faith. . . . The reason we have nothing to say to the contemporary situation is that we have not been thinking about the contemporary situation. We stopped thinking about these things years ago. We stopped thinking Christianly outside the scope of personal morals and personal spirituality. We got into the habit of stepping out of our Christian garments whenever we stepped mentally into the field of social and political life. Because the subject was social or political, we left our well-tried and well-grounded Christian concepts behind us, and adopted the vocabulary of secularism. We put aside talk of vocation, or God's providence, or man's spiritual destiny, and instead chattered with the rest about productivity, assembly-line psychology, and the deployment of personnel. Most ironical of all, we thought we were really being down-to-earth, practical Christians when we went in for this kind of thing.[4]

In contrast to this confusion, there is another way to deal with our calling to be God's people for a society in peril. There is a choice between capitulation and accommodation on the one hand and withdrawal or world-flight on the other. A new way is emerging that is rooted in biblical orthodoxy, is able to be self-critical, and is, in a creative sense, ecumenical.

As a point of departure, there are two illustrations. In 1986 the National Association of Evangelicals passed a resolution entitled "Go . . . Liberate." It stated:

The message of salvation also includes the announcement of God's kingdom. God's saving intent cannot be detached from his lordship over creation and history. The ultimate opponents of God's purpose are the principalities and powers under Satan, the prince of darkness. Salvation includes vindication of God's justice. Though liberation is fundamentally spiritual and personal, it is also cultural. God's righteousness will be vindicated in the final coming of his kingdom. In the meantime, God's rule is not in abeyance. He curbs rebellion by partial judgment. Above all, he calls upon church to speak out against slavery—spiritual, social, economic—whether that slavery is due to personal sins, the sins of others, or materialistic social structures. Our proclamation of the gospel though primarily personal and spiritual is also the proclamation of the rights of God in the social, political, and cultural systems of our day. Liberation must never be cut off from its specific and proper roots in the gospel of the kingdom of God. It must never be merely politicized nor simply spiritualized.[5]

Many evangelicals who have been individualistic and opposed to a social dimension of the gospel are changing.

The Roman Catholic community has expressed something of the same thing, for example, at Vatican Council II:

All that goes to make up the temporal order—personal and family values, culture, economic interests, the trades and professions, institutions of the political community, international relations, and so on, as well as their gradual development—all these are not merely helps to man's last end: they possess a value of their own, placed in them by God, whether considered individually or as parts of the integral temporal structure: "And God saw all that he had made and found it very good" (Gn 1:31). This natural goodness of theirs receives an added dignity from their relation with the human person, for whose use they have been created. And then, too, God has willed to gather together all that was natural, all that was supernatural, into a single whole in Christ, "so that in everything he would have the primacy" (Col 1:18). Far from depriving the temporal order of its autonomy, of its specific ends, of its own laws and resources, or its importance for human well-being, this design, on the contrary, increases its energy and excellence, raising it at the same time to the level of man's integral vocation here below. . . . It is the work of the entire church to fashion men able to establish the proper scale of values in the temporal order and direct it towards God through Christ. Pastors have the duty to set forth clearly the principles concerning the purpose of creation and the use to be made of the world, and to provide moral and spiritual helps for the renewal of the temporal order in Christ. Laymen ought to take on themselves as their distinctive task this renewal of the temporal order. Guided by the light of the gospel and the mind of the church, promoted by Christian love, they should act in this domain in a direct way and in their own specific manner. As citizens among citizens they must bring to their cooperation with others their own special competence, and act on their own responsibility; everywhere and always they have to seek the justice of the kingdom of God. The temporal order is to be renewed in such a way that, while its own principles are fully respected, it is harmonized with the principles of the Christian life and adapted to the various conditions of times, places, and peoples. Among the tasks of this apostolate, Christian social action is preeminent. The Council desires to see it extend today to every sector of life, not forgetting the cultural sphere.[6]

Is a new openness emerging to a biblically based, holistic Christian faith that addresses work, culture, to politics? In order to encourage such a development, let us now turn to a biblical pattern for a Christian community that will make a difference in work, culture, and politics.

Humanity's Cultural Task

The opening chapters of Genesis establish some of the central norms for the people of God. Genesis 1 and 2 set before us the truth that creation is good and that humans are called to give shape to that creation. We are created images of God, which means we are copies as close to the real thing as possible but not the real thing. God was a worker, and so are we. So we are not slaves to the gods or servants of ourselves, but are called to serve God and our fellow image bearers in the midst of the creation. Work and culture, and thus the political task, are built into human nature as ordinances of God. So the fullness of our calling can be expressed as fully at the lathe as in the pulpit, in the legislature as at the altar.

Some definitions may be helpful. By politics is meant the ordering of our public lives as we live together. Culture and work are almost synonymous. Culture is any human effort expended on the universe to unearth its riches and bring them into the service of our fellow humans for their enrichment and for the glory of God.[7] Culture is not an effete view of musical style but any activity that seeks to unlock the potential of God's creation or to understand or harness its resources.

Of course the Bible emphatically teaches us that work, culture, and politics have been perverted and twisted by sin. As a result, throughout history humankind has tied its happiness to economic, cultural, or political solutions. Rather than service and enrichment, many aim at self-fulfillment and self-aggrandizement. Success or failure at the workplace has become for many the only hope. Such views are evidence of the curse on work. All work and culture is part of our call, but it is not at the heart of our calling. The whole of life is to be lived as a response to God, who is now manifest in Christ and redeems us from sin and restores the image of God in us.

The reality of the curse on work, culture, and politics brings us to our calling as God's people. God said to rebellious Adam, "By the sweat of your brow you will eat your food" (Gn 3:19). That is why the Second Adam sweated blood drops in Gethsemane. Christ comes to redeem us in all the dimensions of life, including work, culture, and politics. When we receive him by faith, he dwells in us and enables us to "do all for the glory of God" (1 Cor 10:31). Those who belong to Christ are called to serve at tables precisely because he served. So the call to work, culture, or politics, is first of all a call to Christ. We are "by him and for him and to him." So we must not secularize our calling to work, culture, and politics, nor must we overspiritualize it.

God's Redemptive Calling for His People

It is, therefore, appropriate that we look at three passages that help define something of the community calling and consequent task of God's people. Genesis 12 teaches that our calling as the people of God involves both great privilege and a corporate mission to the nations of the world: "All peoples on earth will be blessed through you" (Gn 12:3). The people of God are not on a tourist excursion or involved in a blessing party. They are a people involved in the world for mission and service. In the biblical context of Genesis 1 and 2, we have seen that mission involves work, politics, and culture.

In Exodus 19 it is clear that the Old Testament people of God are a community energized and defined by their redemption. Their identity was not in the Egyptian empire but in their calling to be the people of God. They would be energized and defined by the memory that "I am the Lord your God who brought you out of the land of Egypt, the house of bondage." Clearly the purpose of Moses was not simply the freeing of a little band of slaves who would escape from this despotic empire, but a work that was nothing less than an assault on the consciousness of the empire. "Their calling was aimed at nothing less than a dismantling of the empire both in its social practices and its mythic pretensions."[8] God called his people not just to a new religion or a new freedom, though these were essential, but also to the emergence of a new social community. It was an intentional forming of a people who were to go through an enculturation process formed by God's word.

Exodus 19 and 1 Peter 2 are a charter for the people of God. Israel was a genuine alternative community. Moses made a radical break with the social and political realities of the Pharaohs. The gods of Egypt had legitimated that social order. But the people of God were to see by the exodus and its remembrance that the presumed gods were no gods, and the presumed powers were no powers. One of the common phrases of Exodus 19 and 1 Peter 2 that makes this point is "holy nation." The Israel of the Old Testament was a holy nation; the people of God in the New Testament are, in Christ's redemption, given the same charter. A nation is a community of people with a common culture and heritage and allegiance to the same political authority. That powerful metaphor communicates vividly, for it is a *holy* nation. Thus the allegiance is to *God* and the authority is *his word*. It implies a mediatorial rule by the "national" priests, judges, prophets, kings that points to *the* Priest, Prophet, Judge, and King—Jesus Christ. Therefore the gospel re-orders our previous loyalties and commitments. It brings us into an alternative community, and thus no other institution can claim absolute loyalty.

There is not space here to completely unpack Peter's use of this vivid metaphor. But the Old Testament pattern of Exodus wilderness wandering, exile, and occupation, enables us to understand Peter's use of the phrase, "holy nation." In the opening verse of the epistle he addresses his readers as the "exiles of the dispersion" (1 Pt 1:1). The point is that when Israel was dispersed, she did not lose her identity. The status of the people of God in a surrounding alien culture is that they are God's people. This theme of the Christian community as a community in exile runs throughout the New Testament. Much of the instruction of God's people is based on the pattern of slavery, wandering, exile, and occupation (for example, Hebrews 11). We have a new citizenship, a new nationhood. Having been freed from our sin, we now serve him in exile, waiting for the occupation of the new heaven and the new earth.

The important point of this language then is the need for the Christian community to see that its ultimate loyalty is to the kingdom of God. We must not be completely at home in this present order. That is precisely why Peter says in verse 11, "as aliens and exiles ... abstain from the passions of the flesh." The phrase refers not simply to bodily urges but to the *zeitgeist*—a way of thinking and living dominated by the spirit of this present order of things. In that culture we are commanded to do "good deeds" (verse 12). The biblical, theological background to that command rests in Romans 13:1-7, 1 Timothy 2:1-4, and Titus 3:1-8, where the phrase "good deeds" deals directly with the relationship of Christians to the institutions of the secular society. The focus of that phrase "good deeds" is most likely formed by Jeremiah 29:1, 4-9:

> This is the text of the letter that the prophet Jeremiah sent from Jerusalem to the surviving elders among the exiles and to the priests, the prophets, and all the other people Nebuchadnezzar had carried into exile from Jerusalem to Babylon. . . . This is what the Lord Almighty, the God of Israel, says to all those I carried into exile from Jerusalem to Babylon: 'Build houses and settle down; plant gardens and eat what they produce. Marry and have sons and daughters; find wives for your sons and give your daughters in marriage, so that they too may have sons and daughters. Increase in number there; do not decrease. Also, seek the peace and prosperity of the city to which I have carried you into exile. Pray to the Lord for it, because if it prospers, you too will prosper.' Yes, this is what the Lord Almighty, the God of Israel says: 'Do not let the prophets and diviners among you deceive you. Do not listen to the dreams you encourage them to have. They are prophesying lies to you in my name. I have not sent them,' declares the Lord."

So God says: "Take your Christian citizenship seriously. Actively seek the welfare of the city. But at the same time do not be misled by false thinking or engaged in the superstitious practices of the surrounding culture."

Peter concludes the thought by stressing the nature of the good deeds. They will only be shown to be good "in the day of visitation" (1 Pt 2:12). Thus the good deeds are not mere submission or simply prayer. But they are not revolution either. Peter says "live as free men" (1 Pt 2:16). Neither the culture nor the government has ultimate claim on the Christian. Clearly then anarchy is not an option, but neither are we to ape the culture in either values or life style. "[Do not use] your freedom as a pretext for evil; but live as servants of God" (1 Pt 2:16).⁹

The imperative of Scripture is, therefore, that God's priestly and prophetic people are called not to spectacular acts of crusading but to offering their own alternative way of perceiving and living. We are called to lovingly confront the peoples of the world by letting them see their history in the light of God's redemptive freedom. Bringing God's word to the world involves not only proclamation and deeds of mercy but a community of servants. The community of God's people must "speak their life together." Our message must be: "The dominant consciousness of an alien world has no final claim on us, and we have hope for the future." Thus the community stands as God's invitation to an alternative consciousness, a hope for a blessed future when he comes again.

The secular sociologists L.P. Gerlach and V.H. Hine have pointed out that community and group dynamics do at least three things for the people who join: (1) provide a cognitive reorientation, (2) facilitate the development of group ties (esprit de corps), and (3) encourage fulfillment of the expectation of the group norms.¹⁰ These social scientists have discovered a dynamic stamped on human life precisely because of this biblical norm of community, or nationhood. God's people are a counter community with a counter-consciousness and a new reality. That alternative community is the place of beginning to bring change to a society in peril.

Implications of Peoplehood

If we are to be that kind of alternative community, there are a series of attitudes and responses that we need to repent of.

1. **Spiritualizing issues.** It has been the tendency of theologically conservative Christians to divide between the soul and the body, the spiritual and the physical, the spiritual and the social. The Bible knows no such dualism. Beyond that, we often say that all we need to do is to change people's hearts, and that will change society. The Bible speaks of both the individual and the social dimension that must be changed.

2. **World-Flight.** We have often been guilty of withdrawing from the world rather than seeking to be salt and light. Our metaphor has often been a ghetto rather than a beachhead or a launching pad for the building of God's kingdom.

3. **Individualism and Privatism.** As I have already implied, we have used phrases like "personal faith, personal piety." The problem is that personal has come to mean all that is left of self after all that is practical, social, cultural, and political has been removed. But the religion of the Bible is holistic.

4. **The Eschatology Trap.** For many of us, especially within the evangelical community, eschatology is a big issue. Many views have resulted in a gospel that all but destroys social concern or a rapture that gets us off a world that we can let go to hell. The Catholic Christian eschatological confession has simply been that he is coming in a visible return to consummate his kingdom. In the meantime we must work and pray—"Your kingdom come, your will be done, on earth as it is in heaven."

5. **Parochialism.** The purpose of the Allies for Faith and Renewal conference is to say that we have been too divided. We are involved in a missionary confrontation with the culture. We will be ineffective in that confrontation if we are just a collection of groups with our varying private opinions. Even the Protestant Reformers sought "to restore the face of the Catholic church."

It is my proposal that cross-denominational, kingdom-oriented groups be organized to think, pray, and study about being a Christian on the job. Should there be some kind of Christian labor union? How about organizing Christian voting associations to think Christianly about politics and to develop public policy? These should not be romantic civil religion associations looking to return to a Christian America. Nor should they bash the outsiders in the American religious debate. But we must seek to bring our rationally defended, passionately held, biblically based convictions, expressed with civility, into the public square.

Examples from a Few Christian Traditions

In the history of the church there were often co-ecclesial, transdenominational groups organized for the purpose of mutual support and encouragement and focused on a holistic witness to the world. When that was the case there was significant amelioration in work, culture, and politics. There seem to be at least three constants in each situation:

—A group of believers who are separate from, though almost always intimately related to, the normal ecclesiastical function of the church and who are seeking to bring change to church and culture.

—A deeply disciplined study of theology, Scripture, and cultural issues.

—Powerful biblical preaching.

This writer may be guilty of what Herbert Butterfield called "Whig historiography," that is, reading his own prejudices into the events of history. The general conclusions of the material has been checked with some of my own colleagues at Geneva College and with two seminary church historians. There is at least some comfort in having fellow Whigs.

We begin with our Catholic heritage and the mendicant orders that developed in the thirteenth century. They were involved in a vigorous attempt to bring reformation to church and society. There are two marvelous illustrations among many. The Franciscans were not a cloistered community in the remote regions, but they went purposely to the cities that were then emerging. These friars were not bound to one convent with a vow of stability, because they were to be "in the world." From that early time until now there has been a third order of lay Franciscans who take a limited vow and continue to live and work in the world while still a part of the Franciscan community. The Dominicans had a similar purpose. Dominic rather than Wesley may have been the first one to speak of the "world as his parish." Marshal Baldwin speaking of the Franciscans and Dominicans says: "In all cases the rule enjoined some activity outside the cloister or convent. . . . The friars [were] dedicated to an active rather than cloistered life."[11] The focus of these two mendicant movements and others, like the Carmelites, was to bring reformation to a church and society in peril.

We do not need detailed documentation that at the heart of these movements was a commitment to found schools of theology and culture. We simply need to be reminded that out of the bosom of these movements emerged Thomas Aquinas and others like him, and such outward-focused theological writing as *Summa Contra Gentiles.* Add to that the record of the vigorous and powerful preaching of many of the leaders of these movements, which was especially true in the dynamic of their early ministry. Francis' preaching was described as "penetrating the heart like fire." The Dominicans were noted for their preaching in the market place. Many historians have concluded that it was these movements that brought a measure of robust moral life to much of church and society in the thirteenth century.[12]

Two illustrations from the Protestant church will suffice. The powerful preaching and the theological writing and thinking of the early roots of the Wesleyan movement have been well documented. But many have argued that the genius of the Wesleyan impact on church and society in the late eighteenth and early nineteenth centuries was their "class meeting." "It was a weekly gathering, a subdivision of the society at which members were required to give account to one another of their discipleship and thereby sustain each other in witness. These meetings were regarded by Wesley himself as the 'sinews of the movement,' the means by which members watched over one another in love and thus were the light and salt of the world."[13] One of the central purposes of the class meeting was the application and the review of the preaching—the truth of Scripture applied to the calling and life of the people.

The Presbyterian and Reformed tradition is also full of illustrations of this threefold pattern focused on small communities. At various points in history these co-ecclesial movements were called "society meetings," "conventicles," "the exercise." In the early nineteenth century in Scotland, one branch of Presbyterianism developed a printed directory for the weekly meeting of societies. Their purpose was to give "full scope unto the communion of saints and to realize the advantages and pleasures to be derived therefrom."[14] They believed that such "small, select societies" appear to be required by the word of God.[15] Furthermore, this private social gathering would "enliven and encourage you in domestic society, direct you in secular vocations . . . [and it will] promote the improvement of public institutions."[16] Thus an essential purpose of these lay gatherings was to "promote steadfastness and zeal in the public cause of Christ."[17] Clearly matters of work and politics were part of what was discussed. "Views of God's providence in the affairs of nations and influence for the sake of the kingdom of Christ on the nation comport well with the nature of these associations."[18] The zeal for powerful and biblical preaching in these Presbyterian and

Reformed churches, as well as their deep theological writing and thinking, has been well documented. An essential ingredient of renewal and reformation in church and society in those lands affected by the Reformed and Presbyterian traditions seems to have been significantly fueled by these society or conventicle meetings.

Thus in these scattered examples, we see co-ecclesial, often transdenominational, groups that resulted in a courageous and effective witness for Christ's lordship over work, culture, and politics.

Three Specific Models

Now three specific examples of co-ecclesial, transdenominational associations that impacted work, culture, and politics. In the early nineteenth century in England a group of believers who saw "no light in the Anglican or non-Conformist churches"[19] determined to form a voluntary extra-ecclesiastical society that was later called the Clapham Sect. It involved a marvelous combination of politicians, scholars, and clerics. The most well known "member" was William Wilberforce. Their great purpose was "by free moral suasion, in place of old direct control of state or church [to] . . . effect transformation in British Society."[20] Though they did not live together, they often came together in the Clapham region of London to think, pray, and study. They were inspired by the powerful preaching of the Anglican rectors John and Henry Venn and by John Newton. Wilberforce, their public leader in Parliament, expressed their objective as "the suppression of the slave trade and the reformation of manners."[21] The cabinet meeting of the Clapham group became a place where they thought, wrote, and strategized for the impact of the kingdom of God on England. They believed that there was no ideologically and informationally informed public. So the Clapham group set out to out-think, out-write, and out-strategize the secular opposition. It was a group with as much talent as any cabinet and as much appetite for factual detail as any civil service.[22]

The results provide us with one of the great paradigms of the author's thesis. The slave trade was eliminated. Control or elimination of societal evils such as prostitution, lotteries, bear baiting, Sabbath desecration; a system of restitution and relief for debtors; and the reformation of prison discipline can be traced to the pamphleteering, petitioning, and public policy stance of Clapham. The British and Foreign Bible Society, Robert Raikes and the Sunday School movement, a missionary society for and the actual founding of Sierra Leone as a refuge for freed slaves—all arose from the thinking, strategy, prayer, and action of Clapham.

What about the United States? On February 4, 1863, representatives from eleven Protestant denominations formed an organization later entitled the National Reform Association. It was intended to bring together Christians having various ecclesiastical principles "who are concerned about civil and national life. It seeks to organize all the friends of Christian Civil Government against the encroachments and revolutionary demands of secularism."[23] In later years the organization poured most of its energy into emphasis for a Christian amendment to the United States Constitution. But in its earlier manifestation much writing and policy information centered on ameliorating the results of the national sin of slavery, encouraging Sabbath laws, advocating chaplains in governmental institutions, and legislation encouraging the purity and permanence of the family. By 1890 there were seven district secretaries and organizations in thirty-three states, as well as a national convention with 10,000 in attendance, including Anglicans, Methodists, Presbyterians, and many others as conferees.

The literature written fills volumes, and the activity to influence national political party platforms and state constitutional conventions was impressive. Their magazine, the *Christian Statesman*, exists to this day as the remnant of a failed and now largely moribund organization. Some historians of American religion have argued that much of the emphasis of this organization, though well intended, was misdirected and unrealistic because it failed to take account of the pluralism in American political and social life, as well as the emerging reality of the massive immigration of the late nineteenth and early twentieth centuries.[24] But this was not mere civil religionist thrust. It was a call by Christians to a culture and body politic to repent of systematic sin. It was, though misdirected, an attempt to proclaim a biblical holism to work, culture, and politics.

The final model involves a man who became Prime Minister of the Netherlands. Much like Wilberforce in England, he gathered a community around him. Abraham Kuyper, trained in philosophy and theology, became a pastor in the small town of Beesd in the

Netherlands state church. This young pastor, by his own admission, was unconverted until a young lady shared the gospel with him and he came to a saving faith. All of his intellectual gifts were now given to proclaim the lordship of Christ over all of life.

Kuyper went on to bring significant reformation to the church and to become the editor of a Christian daily newspaper. But we center our attention on two aspects of this remarkable man's ministry. A fledgling Christian political party had been started in the mid-nineteenth century called the Anti-Revolutionary party. In the multiparty system of the Netherlands it was to be the radical opposite of the spirit of the French Revolution. Their cry had been "no masters, no God." Such radical secularism was to be opposed by the Anti-Revolutionary party, which sought to apply God's word to all life. In 1871 Kuyper became the leader of the party and organized "voters clubs" throughout Holland. They were transdenominational organizations of people seeking the will of God for national life. By 1879 the Anti-Revolutionary party had eleven representatives in the second chamber of Parliament. Kuyper's organizational ability and his editorial writing in the national Christian newspaper, *De Standard,* gathered a following to the party.

But Kuyper was concerned that the Christian witness move beyond politics to all of culture. Thus he established a fullfledged university, called the Free University: education must be free from the regulation of both church and state. Thus free it could have a faculty and curriculum that would enable Christian men and women to be taught a Christian perspective on the world and life. Kuyper insisted that it must be a university with the full range of professional schools.

The most remarkable thing about this remarkable man was his organization of a coalition government that resulted in his becoming Prime Minister of the Netherlands from 1901 to 1905. A coalition was established between the Anti-Revolutionary party and the Roman Catholic party. Many of his own supporters called it "a monstrous marriage of Rome and Dordt."[25] The secular community said that it "deserved the contempt of every right-thinking person."[26] But Abraham Kuyper's four years as Prime Minister of the Netherlands stand as a monument to the efforts of small-group transdenominational strategy, study, prayer, and boldness for Christ. The early months of his ministry were engulfed by a nationwide rail strike, the legacy of the previous government. Nevertheless, he was able to erect legislation for the freedom of all religious groups to start their own education systems. Model social legislation in the area of labor was enacted, including limited working hours, regulation of labor conditions, and permission for labor parties to organize. He personally wrote social reform legislation involving insurance for sickness disability and old age. A model colonial policy was instituted that ended exploitation and the opium trade and prepared the colonies for self-government.

We do not have the space to continue this brief survey. But Christians concerned about a society in peril need to study the Kuyper movement as a model of what a Christian community can do to bring reformation to culture, work, and politics. We must also ask, Is the stark secularism and theological Liberalism of the Netherlands one hundred years later the evidence of a failure to aggressively pursue Kuyper's goals? That question needs to be engaged as well.

The thesis of this article is that the Scriptures call us to community, a community that exists as an alternative. It is the church in exile. The community is to foster a countercultural way of thinking and acting in the world. Two essential ingredients must fuel that community: sound and relevant biblical preaching and teaching, and careful Christian scholarship that seeks to relate a Christian world and life view to the issues of culture, work, and politics.

Three Suggestions

In order that we may continue to raise up such groups and enhance Christian penetration of the secular work and civil order, the author makes three suggestions:

1. Could we establish a center for distinctively Christian research and theorizing? This author believes that this must be given the highest priority. The Presbyterian scholar J.G. Machen's words in 1912 are relevant today. "What is today a matter of academic speculation begins tomorrow to move armies and pull down empires."[27] A high-quality research center like the Brookings Institute, or The Humanities Center in North Carolina, could be our goal. Such research would provide expert guidance and testimony on matters of inter-church and public concern. Our scattered, underutilized Christian

scholars are not networking. Without such a forum we will lack Christian wisdom for public application.

2. Could such a think tank develop a distinctively Christian curriculum for the development of a Christian way of thinking and acting in culture, work, and politics for lay people? We can be encouraged by the recent publication of books on Christian world and life view. Now is the time for an ample biblical study curriculum for a Christian view of work and politics.

3. Should we use the model of the Anti-Revolutionary party in the Netherlands and their voting clubs? Is it just a dream that as a result of steps one and two, we could see local Christian transdenominational voting clubs emerge across the nation? It must be our prayer that there would be radical Christian thinking so as to transcend our present social and political prejudices. It will take an immense amount of Christian love and patience with one another, but this author believes we could do it. Then, maybe we will hear God saying to his people, "Well done, good and faithful servants."

NINE

The Psychology of Atheism[1]

Paul Vitz

M Y TITLE, "The Psychology of Atheism," may seem strange. Certainly, my psychological colleagues have found it odd and even, I might add, a little disturbing. After all, psychology, since its founding roughly a century ago, has often focused on the opposite topic, namely, the psychology of religious belief. Indeed, in many respects the origins of modern psychology are intimately bound up with psychologists who explicitly proposed interpretations of belief in God.

William James and Sigmund Freud, for example, were both personally and professionally deeply involved in the topic. Recall *The Will to Believe* by James, as well as his still famous *Varieties of Religious Experience*. These two works are devoted to an attempt at understanding belief as the result of psychological, that is, natural, causes. James might have been sympathetic to religion, but his own position was one of doubt and skepticism, and his writings were part of psychology's general undermining of religious faith. As for Sigmund Freud, his critiques of religion, in particular, Christianity, are well known. For now, it is enough to remember how deeply involved Freud and his thought have been with the question of God and religion.

133

Given the close involvement between the founding of much of psychology and a critical interpretation of religion, it should not be surprising that most psychologists view with some alarm any attempt to propose a psychology of atheism. At the very least, such a project puts many psychologists on the defensive and gives them some taste of their own medicine. Psychologists are always observing and interpreting others. It is high time that some of them learned from their own personal experience what it is like to be put under the microscope of psychological theory and experiment. Regardless, I hope to show that the psychological concepts used quite effectively to interpret religion are two-edged swords that can also be used to interpret atheism. Sauce for the believer is equally sauce for the unbeliever.

Before beginning, however, I wish to make two points bearing on the underlying assumption of my remarks. *First,* I assume that the major barriers to belief in God are not rational but—in a general sense—can be called psychological. I do not wish to offend the philosophers, either believers or nonbelievers, but I am quite convinced that for every person strongly swayed by rational argument there are many, many more affected by nonrational psychological factors.

The human heart—no one can truly fathom it or know all its deceits; but at least it is the proper task of the psychologist to try. Thus, to begin, I propose that neurotic psychological barriers to belief in God are of great importance. What some of these might be I will mention shortly. For believers, therefore, it is important to keep in mind that psychological motives and pressures that one is often unaware of often lie behind unbelief.

One of the earliest theorists of the unconscious, St. Paul, wrote, "I can will what is right, but I cannot do it. . . . I see in my members another law at war with the law of my mind" (Rom 7:18, 23). Thus, it seems to me sound theology as well as sound psychology that psychological factors can be impediments to belief as well as behavior, and that these may often be unconscious factors as well. Further, as a corollary, it is reasonable to propose that people vary greatly in the extent to which these factors are present in their lives. Some of us have been blessed with an upbringing, a temperament, a social environment, and other gifts that have made belief in God a much easier thing than for many who have suffered more or have been raised in a spiritually impoverished environment or have had other difficulties with which to cope. Scripture makes it clear that many children—even into the third or fourth generation—suffer from the sins of their fathers, including the sins of fathers who may have been believers. In short, my first point is that some people have much more serious psychological barriers to belief than others, a point consistent with the Scriptures' clear statement that we are not to judge others, however much we are called to correct evil.

My *second* point as qualification is that in spite of serious difficulties to belief, all of us still have a free choice to accept God or reject him. This qualification is not in contradiction to the first. Perhaps a little elaboration will make this clearer. One person, as a consequence of his particular past, present environment, and so on, may find it much harder than most people to believe in God. But presumably, at any moment, certainly at many times, he can choose to move toward God or to move away. One man may start with so many barriers that even after years of slowly choosing to move toward God he may still not be there. Some may die before they reach belief. We assume they will be judged—like all of us—on how far they traveled toward God and how well they loved others—on how well they did with what they had. Likewise, another man without psychological difficulties at all is still free to reject God, and no doubt many do so. Thus, although the ultimate issue is one of the will and our sinful nature, it is still possible to investigate those psychological factors that predispose one to unbelief, that make the road to belief in God especially long and hard.

Social and Personal Motives

There seems to be a widespread assumption throughout much of the Western intellectual community that belief in God is based on all kinds of irrational, immature needs and wishes, but atheism or skepticism is derived from a rational, no-nonsense appraisal of the way things really are. To begin a critique of this assumption, I start with my own case history.

As some of you know, after a rather weak, wishy-washy Christian upbringing, I became an atheist in college in the 1950s and remained so throughout graduate school and my first years as a young experimental psychologist on the faculty at New York University.

That is, I am an adult converter, more technically, a reconvert to Christianity who came back to the faith, much to his surprise, in my late thirties in the very secular environment of academic psychology in New York City.

I am not going into this to bore you with my life story, but to note that through reflection on my own experience it is now clear to me that my reasons for becoming and remaining an atheist-skeptic from about age 18 to 38 were superficial, irrational, and largely without intellectual or moral integrity. Furthermore, I am convinced that my motives were, and still are, commonplace today among intellectuals, especially social scientists.

The major factors involved in my becoming an atheist—although I was not really aware of them at the time—were as follows.

General socialization. An important influence on me in my youth was a significant social unease. I was somewhat embarrassed to be from the Midwest, for it seemed terribly dull, narrow, and provincial. There was certainly nothing romantic or impressive about being from Cincinnati, Ohio, and from a vague mixed German-English-Swiss background. It was all terribly middle class. Further, besides escape from a dull, and according to me unworthy, socially embarrassing past, I wanted to take part in, in fact to be comfortable in, the new, exciting, even glamorous, secular world into which I was moving. I am sure that similar motives have strongly influenced the lives of countless upwardly mobile young people in the last two centuries. Consider Voltaire, who moved into the glittery, aristocratic, sophisticated world of Paris, and who always felt embarrassed about his provincial and nonaristocratic origin; or the Jewish ghettos that so many assimilating Jews have fled; or the latest young arrival in New York, embarrassed about his fundamentalist parents. This kind of socialization pressure has pushed many away from belief in God and all that this belief is associated with for them.

I remember a small seminar in graduate school where almost every member there at some time expressed this kind of embarrassment and response to the pressures of socialization into "modern life." One student was trying to escape his Southern Baptist background, another a small town Mormon environment, a third was trying to get out of a very Jewish Brooklyn ghetto, and the fourth was me.

Specific socialization. Another major reason for my wanting to become an atheist was that I desired to be accepted by the powerful and influential scientists in the field of psychology. In particular, I wanted to be accepted by my professors in graduate school. As a graduate student I was thoroughly socialized by the specific "culture" of academic research psychology. My professors at Stanford, however much they might disagree on psychological theory, were, as far as I could tell, united in only two things—their intense personal career ambition and their rejection of religion. As the psalmist says, "The man greedy for gain curses and renounces the Lord. In the pride of his countenance the wicked does not seek him; all his thoughts are, 'There is no God'" (Ps 10:3-4).

In this environment, just as I had learned how to dress like a college student by putting on the right clothes, I also learned to "think" like a proper psychologist by putting on the right—that is, atheistic—ideas and attitudes.

Personal convenience. Finally, in this list of superficial but nevertheless strong irrational pressures to become an atheist, I must list simple personal convenience. The fact is that it is quite inconvenient to be a serious believer in today's powerful secular and neopagan world. I would have had to give up many pleasures and a good deal of time.

Without going into details it was not hard to imagine the sexual pleasures that would have to be rejected if I became a serious believer. And then I also knew it would cost me time and some money. There would be church services, church groups, time for prayer and Scripture reading, time spent helping others. I was already too busy. Obviously, becoming religious would be a real inconvenience.

Now perhaps you think that such reasons are restricted to especially callow young men—like me in my twenties. However, such reasoning is not so restricted. Here I will take up the case of Mortimer Adler, a well-known American philosopher, writer, and intellectual who spent much of his life thinking about God and religious topics. One of his books is entitled, *How to Think about God: A Guide for the 20th-Century Pagan.*[2] In this work, Adler presses the argument for the existence of God very strongly, and by the latter chapters he is very close to accepting the living God. Yet he pulls back and remains among "the vast company of the religiously uncommitted." But Adler leaves the impression that this decision is more one of will than of intellect, as one of his reviewers notes.[3] Adler confirms this impression in his autobiography, *Philosopher at Large*.[4] There, while investigating his reasons for twice stopping short of a full religious commitment, he writes that the answer "lies in the state of one's will, not in the state of one's mind." Adler goes on to comment that to become seriously religious "would require a radical change in my way of life" and "the simple truth of the matter is that I did not wish to live up to being a genuinely religious person."

There you have it: a remarkably honest and conscious admission that being "a genuinely religious person" would be too much trouble, too inconvenient. I cannot but assume that such are the shallow reasons behind many an unbeliever's position.

In summary, because of my social needs to assimilate, because of my professional needs to be accepted as part of academic psychology, and because of my personal needs for a convenient life style—for all these needs atheism was simply the best policy. Looking back on these motives, I can honestly say that a return to atheism has all the appeal of a return to adolescence.

Psychoanalytic Motives

As is generally known, the central Freudian criticism of belief in God is that such a belief is untrustworthy because of its psychological origin. That is, God is a projection of our own intense, unconscious desires; he is a wish fulfillment derived from childish needs for protection and security. Since these wishes are largely unconscious, any denial of such an interpretation is to be given little credence. It should be noted that in developing this kind of critique, Freud has raised the *ad hominem* argument to one of wide influence. It is in *The Future of an Illusion* (1927) that Freud makes his position clearest:

> [R]eligious ideas have arisen from the same needs as have all the other achievements of civilization: from the necessity of defending oneself against the crushing superior force of nature. (p. 21)

Therefore, religious beliefs are

> illusions, fulfillments of the oldest, strongest, and most urgent wishes of mankind. . . . As we already know, the terrifying

impressions of helplessness in childhood Karoused the need for protection—for protection through love—which was provided by the father.... Thus the benevolent rule of a divine Providence allays our fear of the danger of life. (p. 30)

Let us look at this argument carefully, for in spite of the enthusiastic acceptance of it by so many uncritical atheists and skeptics, it is really a very weak position.

In the first paragraph Freud fails to note that his arguments against religious belief are, in his own words, equally valid against *all* the achievements of civilization, including psychoanalysis itself. That is, if the psychic origin of an intellectual achievement invalidates its truth value, then physics, biology, much more psychoanalysis itself, are vulnerable to the same charge.

In the second paragraph Freud makes another strange claim, namely that the oldest and most urgent wishes of mankind are for the loving protecting guidance of a powerful loving father, for divine Providence. However, if these wishes were as strong and ancient as he claims, one would expect pre-Christian religions to have strongly emphasized God as a benevolent father. In general, this was far from the case for the pagan religions of the Mediterranean world—and is still not the case for such popular religions as Buddhism and for much of Hinduism. Indeed, Judaism and most especially Christianity are in many respects distinctive in their emphasis on God as a loving father.

However, let us put these two intellectual gaffes aside and turn to another understanding of Freud's projection theory. It can be shown that this theory is not really an integral part of psychoanalysis—and, thus cannot claim fundamental support from psychoanalytic theory. It is essentially an autonomous argument. Actually, Freud's critical attitude toward and rejection of religion is rooted in his personal predilections and is a kind of meta-psychoanalysis, or background framework, which is not well connected to his more specifically clinical concepts. (This separation or autonomy with respect to most psychoanalytic theory very likely accounts for its influence outside of psychoanalysis.) There are two pieces of evidence for this interpretation of the projection theory.

The first is that this theory had been clearly articulated many years earlier by Ludwig Feuerbach in his book *The Essence of Christianity*

(1841). Here are some representative quotes from Feuerbach which make this clear:

> What man misses—whether this be an articulate and therefore-conscious, or an unconscious, need—that is his God.

> Man projects his nature into the world outside himself before he finds it in himself.

> To live in projected dream-images is the essence of religion. Religion sacrifices reality to the projected dream.

Many other quotes could be provided in which Feuerbach describes religion in "Freudian" terms such as wish-fulfillment, and so on.

Feuerbach's interpretation was well-known in European intellectual circles, and Freud, as a youth, read Feuerbach avidly.[5] What Freud did with this argument was to revive it in a more eloquent form, and publish it at a later time when the audience desiring to hear such a theory was much larger. And, of course, it was implied that somehow the findings and theory of psychoanalysis gave the theory strong support. The Feuerbachian character of Freud's *Illusion* position is also demonstrated by such notions as "the crushing superior force of nature" and "the terrifying impression of helplessness in childhood," which are not psychoanalytic in terminology or in meaning.

The other piece of evidence for the non-psychoanalytic basis of the projection theory comes directly from Freud, who explicitly says so himself. In a letter of 1927 to his friend Oskar Pfister (an early psychoanalyst, and believing Protestant pastor), Freud wrote:

> Let us be quite clear on the point that the views expressed in my book (*The Future of an Illusion*) form no part of analytic theory. They are my personal views.[6]

There is one other somewhat different interpretation of belief in God which Freud also developed, but although this has a very modest psychoanalytic character, it is really an adaptation of Feuerbachian projection theory. This is Freud's relatively neglected interpretation of the ego ideal. The superego, including the ego ideal, is the "heir of the Oedipus complex," representing a projection of an idealized father—and presumably God the father.[7]

The difficulty here is that the ego ideal did not really receive great attention or development within Freud's writings. Furthermore, it is easily interpreted as an adoption of Feuerbach's projection theory. Thus, we can conclude that psychoanalysis does not in actuality provide significant theoretical concepts for characterizing belief in God as neurotic. Freud either used Feuerbach's much older projection or illusion theory, or incorporated Feuerbach in his notion of the ego ideal. Presumably, this is the reason Freud acknowledged to Pfister that his *Illusion* book was not a true part of psychoanalysis.

Atheism as Oedipal Wish-Fulfillment

Nevertheless, Freud is quite right to worry that a belief can be an illusion because it derives from powerful wishes—from unconscious, childish needs. The irony is that he clearly did provide a very powerful, new way to understand the neurotic basis of atheism.[8]

The Oedipus Complex. The central concept in Freud's work, aside from the unconscious, is the now well-known Oedipus complex. In the case of male personality development, the essential features of this complex are the following. Roughly in the age period of three to six the boy develops a strong sexual desire for the mother. At the same time the boy develops an intense hatred and fear of the father, and a desire to supplant him, a "craving for power." This hatred is based on the boy's knowledge that the father, with his greater size and strength, stands in the way of his desire. The child's fear of the father may explicitly be a fear of castration by the father, but more typically, it has a less specific character. The son does not really kill the father, of course, but patricide is assumed to be a common preoccupation of his fantasies and dreams. The "resolution" of the complex is supposed to occur through the boy's recognition that he cannot replace the father, and through fear of castration, which eventually leads the boy to identify with the father, to identify with the aggressor, and to repress the original frightening components of the complex.

It is important to keep in mind that, according to Freud, the Oedipus complex is never truly resolved, and is capable of activation at later periods—almost always, for example, at puberty. Thus the powerful ingredients of murderous hate and of incestuous sexual desire within a family context are never in fact removed. Instead, they are covered over and repressed. Freud expresses the neurotic potential of this situation:

> The Oedipus-complex is the actual nucleus of neuroses. . . . What remains of the complex in the unconscious represents the disposition to the later development of neuroses in the adult.[9]

In short, all human neuroses derive from this complex. Obviously, in most cases, this potential is not expressed in any seriously neurotic manner. Instead it shows up in attitudes toward authority, in dreams, slips of the tongue, transient irrationalities, and so on.

Now, in postulating a universal Oedipus complex as the origin of all our neuroses, Freud inadvertently developed a straightforward rationale for understanding the wish-fulfilling origin of rejecting God. After all, the Oedipus complex is unconscious, it is established in childhood and, above all, its dominant motive is hatred of the father and the desire for him not to exist, especially as represented by the desire to overthrow or kill the father. Freud regularly described God as a psychological equivalent to the father, and so a natural expression of Oedipal motivation would be powerful, unconscious desires for the nonexistence of God. Therefore, in the Freudian framework, atheism is an illusion caused by the Oedipal desire to kill the father and replace him with oneself. To act as if God does not exist is an obvious, not so subtle disguise for a wish to kill him, much the same way as in a dream, the image of a parent going away or disappearing can represent such a wish. "God is dead" is simply an undisguised Oedipal wish-fulfillment.

It is certainly not hard to understand the Oedipal character of so much contemporary atheism and skepticism. Hugh Heffner, even James Bond, with their rejection of God plus their countless girls, are so obviously living out Freud's Oedipal and primal rebellion (for example, see *Totem and Taboo*). So are countless other skeptics who live out variations of the same scenario of exploitative sexual permissiveness combined with narcissistic self-worship.

And, of course, the Oedipal dream is not only to kill the father and possess the mother or other women in the group but also to displace him. Modern atheism has attempted to accomplish this. Now man, not God, is the consciously specified ultimate source of goodness and power in the universe. Humanistic philosophies glorify him and his "potential" much the same way religion glorifies the creator. We have progressed from one God to many gods to everyone a god. In essence, man—through his narcissism and Oedipal wishes—has tried to succeed where Satan failed, by seating himself on the throne of God. Thanks to Freud it is now easier to understand the deeply neurotic, thoroughly untrustworthy psychology of this unbelief.

One interesting example of the Oedipal motivation proposed here is that of Voltaire, a leading skeptic about all things religious who denied the Christian and Jewish notion of a personal God—of God as a father. Voltaire was a deist who believed in a cosmic, depersonalized God of unknown character.

The psychologically important thing about Voltaire is that he strongly rejected his father—so much so that he rejected his father's name and took the name "Voltaire." It is not exactly certain where the new name came from but one widely held interpretation is that it was constructed from the letters of his mother's last name. When Voltaire was in his early twenties (in 1718), he published a play entitled *Oedipus* (*Edipe,* 1718), the first of his plays to be publicly performed. The play itself recounts the classic legend with heavy allusions to religious and political rebellion. Throughout his life, Voltaire (like Freud) toyed with the idea that he was not his father's son. He apparently felt the desire to be from a higher, more aristocratic family than his actual middle-class background. (A major expression of this concern with having a more worthy father is the play *Candide*.) In short, Voltaire's hostility to his own father, his religious rejection of God the Father, and his political rejection of the king—an acknowledged father figure—are all reflections of the same basic needs. Psychologically speaking, Voltaire's rebellion against his father and against God are easily interpretable as Oedipal wish-fulfillment, as comforting illusions, and therefore, following Freud, as beliefs and attitudes unworthy of a mature mind.

Diderot, the great Encyclopedist and an avowed atheist—indeed he is one of the founding brothers of modern atheism—also had both Oedipal preoccupation and insight. Freud approvingly quotes

Diderot's anticipatory observation:

> If the little savage were left to himself, preserving all his foolishness and adding to the small sense of a child in the cradle the violent passions of a man of thirty, he would strangle his father and lie with his mother.[10]

The Theory of the Defective Father

I am well aware of the fact that there is good reason to give only limited acceptance to Freud's Oedipal theory. In any case, it is my view that although the Oedipus complex is valid for some, the theory is far from being a universal representation of unconscious motivation. Since there is need for deeper understanding of atheism, and since I do not know of any theoretical framework—except the Oedipal one—I am forced to sketch out a model of my own, or really to develop an undeveloped thesis of Freud. In his essay on Leonardo da Vinci, Freud made the following remark:

> Psychoanalysis, which has taught us the intimate connection between the father complex and belief in God, has shown us that the personal God is logically nothing but an exalted father, and *daily* demonstrates to us how youthful persons lose their religious belief as soon as the authority of the father breaks down.[11]

This statement makes no assumptions about unconscious sexual desires for the mother, or even about presumed universal competitive hatred focused on the father. Instead, Freud makes the simple, easily understandable claim that once a child or youth is disappointed in and loses respect for his or her earthly father, then belief in the heavenly father becomes impossible. There are, of course, many ways that a father can lose his authority and seriously disappoint a child. Some of these ways—for which clinical evidence is given below—are:

1. He can be present but obviously weak, cowardly, and unworthy of respect—even if otherwise pleasant or "nice."

2. He can be present but physically, sexually, or psychologically abusive.

3. He can be absent through death or by abandoning or leaving the family.

Taken all together these proposed determinants of atheism will be called the "defective father" hypothesis. To support the validity of this approach, I will conclude by providing case history material from the lives of prominent atheists, for it was in reading the biographies of atheists that this hypothesis first struck me.

We begin with Sigmund Freud's relationship to his father. That Freud's father, Jacob, was a deep disappointment—or worse—is generally agreed to by his biographers.[12] Specifically, his father was a weak man unable to provide financially for his family. Instead, money for support seems to have been provided by his wife's family and others. Furthermore, Freud's father was passive in response to anti-Semitism. Freud recounts an episode told to him by his father in which Jacob allowed an anti-Semite to call him a dirty Jew and to knock his hat off. Young Sigmund, on hearing the story, was mortified at his father's failure to respond. Sigmund Freud was a complex and in many respects ambiguous man, but all agree that he was a courageous fighter and that he greatly admired courage in others. Sigmund, as a young man, several times stood up physically against anti-Semitism—and, of course, he was one of the greatest intellectual fighters.

Jacob's defects as a father, however, probably go still deeper. Specifically, in two of his letters as an adult, Freud writes that his father was a sexual pervert and that Jacob's own children suffered from this. There are also other possible moral disasters that I have not bothered to note.

The connection of Jacob to God and religion was also present for his son. Jacob was involved in a kind of reform Judaism when Freud was a child, and the two of them spent hours reading the Bible together, and later Jacob became increasingly involved in reading the Talmud and in discussing Jewish Scripture. In short, this weak, rather passive "nice guy," this schlemiel, was clearly connected to Judaism and God, and also to a serious lack of courage and quite possibly to sexual perversion and other weaknesses very painful to young Sigmund.

Very briefly, other famous atheists seem to have had a similar relationship to their fathers. Karl Marx made it clear that he did not respect his father. An important reason for this was that his father converted to Christianity—not out of any religious conviction, but out of a desire to make life easier. He assimilated for convenience. In doing this, Marx's father broke an old family tradition. He was the first in his family who did not become a rabbi; indeed, Karl Marx came from a long line of rabbis on both sides of his family.

Ludwig Feuerbach's father did something that very easily could have deeply hurt his son. When Feuerbach was about 18, his father left his family and openly took up living with another woman in a different town. This was in Germany in the early 1800s, when such a public rejection would have been a scandal and a profound expression of rejection of young Ludwig—and, of course, of his mother and the other children.

Let us jump 100 years or so and look at the life of one of America's best known atheists—Madalyn Murray O'Hair. Here I will quote from her son's book on what life was like in his family when he was a child.[13] The book opens when he is eight years old: "We rarely did anything together as a family. Hatred between my grandfather and mother barred such wholesome scenes." He writes that he really did not know why his mother hated her father so much, but hate him she did, for the opening chapter records a very ugly fight in which she attempted to kill her father with a 10-inch butcher knife. Madalyn failed but screamed, "I'll see you dead. I'll get you yet. I'll walk on your grave!" Whatever the cause of Madalyn O'Hair's intense hatred of her father, it is clear from this book that it was deep and that it went back into her childhood. At least psychological and possibly physical abuse is a plausible cause.[14]

Besides abuse, rejection, or cowardice, a father can be seriously defective simply by not being there. Many children, of course, interpret death of their father as a kind of betrayal or an act of desertion. In this respect it is remarkable that the pattern of a dead father is so common in the lives of many prominent atheists.

Baron d'Holbach (born Paul Henri Thiry), the French rationalist and probably the first public atheist, was apparently an orphan by the age of 13 and living with his uncle, from whom he took the new name Holbach. Bertrand Russell's father died when young Bertrand was four years old; Nietzsche was the same age as Russell when he lost his father; Sartre's father died before Sartre was born; Camus was a year old when he lost his father. Obviously, much more evidence needs to be obtained on the "defective father" hypothesis. But the information already available is substantial; it is unlikely to be an accident.

The psychology of how a dead or nonexistent father could lay an emotional base for atheism might not seem clear at first glance. But, after all, if one's own father is absent or so weak as to die, or so untrustworthy as to desert, then it is not hard to attribute the same weaknesses to one's own heavenly father.

Finally, there is also the early personal experience of suffering, of death, of evil, sometimes combined with anger at God for allowing it to happen. Any early anger at God for the loss of a father and the subsequent suffering is still another and different psychology of unbelief, but one closely related to that of a defective father. Some of this psychology is captured in Russell Baker's autobiography.[15] Russell Baker is the well-known journalist and humorous writer for the New York *Times*. His father was taken to the hospital and died there suddenly when young Russell was only five. Baker wept and sorrowed and spoke to the family housekeeper, Bessie:

> For the first time I thought seriously about God. Between sobs I told Bessie that if God could do things like this to people, then God was hateful and I had no more use of him.
>
> Bessie told me about the peace of Heaven and the joy of being among the angels and the happiness of my father who was already there. The argument failed to quiet my rage.
>
> "God loves us all just like his own children," Bessie said.
>
> "If God loves me, why did he make my father die?"
>
> Bessie said that I would understand someday, but she was only partly right. That afternoon, though I couldn't have phrased it this way then, I decided that God was a lot less interested in people than anybody in Morrisonville was willing to admit. That day I decided that God was not entirely to be trusted.
>
> After that I never cried again with any real conviction, nor expected much of anyone's God except indifference, nor loved deeply without fear that it would cost me dearly in pain. At the age of five I had become a skeptic.

Let me conclude by noting that however prevalent the superficial motives for being an atheist, there still remain in many instances the deep and disturbing psychological sources as well. However easy it may be to state the hypothesis of the "defective father," we must not forget the difficulty, the pain, the complexity that lie behind each individual case. And for those whose atheism has been conditioned by a father who rejected, who denied, who hated, who manipulated, or who physically or sexually abused them, there must be understanding and compassion. Certainly for a child to be forced to hate his own father—or even to despair because of his father's weaknesses—is a great tragedy. After all, the child only wants to love his father. For any unbeliever whose atheism is grounded in such experience, the believer, blessed by God's love, should pray most especially that ultimately father and child will meet in heaven—meet and embrace and experience great joy. If so, perhaps the former atheist will experience even more joy than the believer. For, in addition to the happiness of the believer, the atheist will have that extra increment that comes from his surprise at finding himself surrounded by joy in, of all places, his father's house.

TEN

One-to-One Pastoral Care: Leading Christians to Maturity

by John C. Blattner

S OMETIMES WHEN I THINK BACK ON IT, I am amazed that I survived my spiritual infancy.

I gave my life to Jesus when I was in college, along with a small group of friends. Having been brought up in church-going homes, we had a general idea of the kinds of things one was supposed to do when one became a serious Christian, and we tried our best to do them.

It seemed clear that we should be learning more about Scripture, so we met every week for Bible study. Perhaps I should say we met for Bible *discussion.* None of us knew much about the Bible, so we would just read a chunk of Scripture and talk about it for a while (usually for hours).

We knew we ought to pray, and so we did, both individually during the week and as a group when we got together each week (this could also last quite a while).

Whenever someone ran into a challenge in their life (which, of course, occurred regularly), we would all search the Scriptures and pray and take counsel together about what the right course of action would be (which could easily take us into the wee, small hours—I think it was during this period of my life that I first learned to drink coffee).

Somehow we muddled through to some semblance of stable Christian living. But that happy outcome was by no means a sure thing. How much easier, and safer, our first steps in the faith would have been if we had only had someone a little bit older in the Lord, and a little more experienced in his ways, to guide us.

No doubt many of us have experienced something similar. Over the years we have heard sermons, attended seminars, listened to tapes, read books, pamphlets, and magazine articles about various aspects of Christian living. We have worshiped at worship meetings, prayed at prayer meetings, shared at small group meetings. We have sat on committees and served on service teams. All of it has been helpful, to one degree or another.

Yet our times of most rapid and confident growth have occurred when some wise, patient, loving brother or sister has come alongside and helped us understand what the sermon or tape or article was trying to teach us, has helped us apply that teaching to our particular circumstances, has coached and commended and corrected us—in short, has cooperated with the Lord as a human agent in his efforts to bring us to maturity.

As pastoral leaders, we view the same phenomenon from the other side. We can usually observe that those among the people we lead who have received this kind of personalized attention seem to make more progress in serving the Lord, and to get less bogged down in problems and difficulties.

But there are never enough such people. One-to-one help tends to be a hit-or-miss proposition in most of our churches and groups. Whether a given individual receives such help usually depends on whether he happens to know someone who happens to have the ability and inclination to serve him in this way. If only we could provide pastoral care of this sort to all our people!

Well, perhaps we *can* do just that. Here I would like to explain what one-to-one pastoral care is (and is not), how it works in practice, and how it can be incorporated into the life of a church.

The New Testament offers several glimpses of one-to-one pastoral care—that is, of a more experienced individual helping a younger person or group attain and maintain Christian maturity and fruit-fulness.

The most exalted example, of course, is that of Jesus and the Twelve. But the fact that it is exalted does not mean it is any less helpful as a model for us today. Jesus focused his pastoral care—and multiplied his ministry—by concentrating his effort on a handful of men even as he continued to minister to the masses. I do not think it is presumptuous for us to learn from, and even imitate to some degree, his method.

Paul's relationship with Timothy is often viewed as an instance of one-to-one pastoral care. Paul had a number of *colleagues* in the ministry, Silas and Barnabas notable among them. But Timothy appears to have been more than a colleague. He was a *disciple* of Paul's, a man younger both in years and in the faith, who apprenticed himself to Paul for the sake of growth in personal maturity and ministry. Paul addresses some people in his letters as "coworkers" and "yokefellows"; he addresses Timothy as "my true son in the faith" (see Acts 16:1-5; 1 Timothy 1:2).

That Paul meant for his relationship with Timothy to be used as a model for pastoral relationships in the church is implied in the advice he gave his protégé: "You then, my son, be strong in the grace that is in Christ Jesus. And the things you have heard me say in the presence of many witnesses entrust to reliable men who will also be qualified to teach others" (2 Tm 2:1-2).

In our own day, the importance of one-to-one pastoral care as a means to leading Christians to maturity is championed by the parachurch ministry, the Navigators. The Navigators speak frequently of the importance of discipleship, by which they mean the basic process of helping Christians become solidly grounded in faith and practice (as opposed to a more extensive "discipleship" consisting of total-life formation). Author LeRoy Eims, in *The Lost Art of Disciple-Making,* explains:

> What, then, is the problem today? Why are fruitful, dedicated, mature disciples so rare? The biggest reason is that all too often we have relied on programs or materials or some other thing to do the job.
>
> The ministry is to be carried on by people, not programs. It is to

be carried out by some*one* and not by some*thing*. Disciples cannot be mass-produced. We cannot drop people into a "program" and see disciples emerge at the end of the production line. It takes time to make disciples. It takes individual, personal attention. It takes hours of prayer for them. It takes patience and understanding to teach them how to get into the word of God for themselves, how to feed and nourish their souls, and by the power of the Holy Spirit how to apply the word to their lives. And it takes being an example to them in all of the above.

I am sure that Eims would not simply dismiss programs, materials, and other things as totally without value. He argues, rather, that by themselves they are not enough. They leave out the ingredient of one-to-one pastoral care, which is indispensable to helping Christians grow to maturity.

By one-to-one pastoral care, I simply mean a relationship in which one person helps another person grow to a basic level of maturity and fruitfulness in the Christian life.

The concrete expression of a one-to-one pastoral care relationship is a regular meeting between the individual and the pastoral worker to talk about how the individual's life is going, where the current challenges lie, what areas the pastoral worker feels might be in need of attention.

How often do they meet? Often enough for the pastoral worker to know how the individual is doing in his spiritual life, in his responsibilities to his family and his job, and in his Christian service; and often enough to be able to address problems and difficulties in a timely manner. Once a month is not a bad starting point, though there are exceptions:

• Those new in the Christian life benefit from more frequent attention—perhaps weekly—because they are learning and changing so much in the early stages.

• Those who are going through some particularly difficult or demanding life experience (anything from unemployment to dealing with a flare-up of serious wrongdoing to making a decision to get married) also benefit from more frequent attention.

• The pastoral worker will want to give more frequent attention to those in whose lives he senses the Lord to be particularly active at the moment, those to whom he is giving more extensive character formation, and those he is training for some particular arena of service.

• Some people, having attained a basic level of Christian maturity and fruitfulness, are able to sustain themselves and continue to grow with minimal ongoing personal attention. A pastoral worker might meet with such a person only a few times a year or when specific needs and questions arise.

Most people will continue to need, or at least to benefit substantially from, regular (approximately monthly) contact on an indefinite basis.

The Pastoral Agenda

When the pastoral worker and the individual do get together, what precisely do they talk about?

The obvious starting point is simply to get an update on how the person is doing and to address whatever he or she is currently experiencing as a need or problem. The pastoral worker might begin by asking, "What's the Lord been doing in your life lately?" or "Is there anything you wanted to bring up at our meeting today?" He can then listen carefully and either offer input on the spot or suggest that they tackle a particular area in greater depth at a later time.

But one-to-one care is most effective when the pastoral worker operates in the *pro*active rather than the *re*active mode, that is, when he takes the initiative and pursues an agenda of his own rather than merely responding to the individual's felt needs. Problem-solving is important, but a person's problems will not usually mark the straightest path to Christian maturity.

What should such a pastoral agenda look like? What are the areas that the pastoral worker should touch on regularly, looking for weaknesses to be strengthened, strengths to be enhanced, and new steps forward to be taken? A complete list would be impossibly long and would vary from one person to the next based on individual weaknesses, strengths, and callings. Here is a short list of topics.

Prayer. Is he praying regularly? experiencing any particular problems or breakthroughs in prayer? hearing the Lord speak to him? responding to what he hears?

Study. Is he reading, studying, and meditating on Scripture in a regular way? understanding what he reads? applying it in his own life? Is he augmenting his Scripture study with other spiritual reading, tapes, and so on?

Righteousness. Is he living a life worthy of the gospel? obeying the commandments? dealing with those areas of temptation, weakness, and wrongdoing that are particularly troublesome in his own life?

Family. Is he serving effectively as spiritual head of the home? loving and caring for his wife? safeguarding communication time with her? providing spiritual and practical direction for her life? Are he and his wife taking proper initiative in raising their children for the Lord? disciplining them? spending quality time with them? Are they effectively overseeing the family's spiritual life? schedule? use of media?

Service. Is he regularly reaching out in service to his brothers and sisters in the Lord? sharing the gospel with others? giving of himself to help the needy? actively engaging in service within the church or group?

Fellowship. Is he building up the life of the group by faithfully participating in its key activities? actively developing personal relationships with other members apart from formal activities? dealing with ruptures in relationships as they occur?

Time Use. Is he ordering his priorities responsibly? allocating his time so that high-priority concerns are covered first? using a personal schedule to ensure his reliability?

Finances. Is he a faithful steward of the resources the Lord has entrusted to him? Is he tithing? giving alms? being generous in blessing and supporting those around him? Is he using a written budget to ensure that his spending lines up with godly principles and with his level of income?

Job Responsibilities. Is he rendering service to his employer as to the Lord? keeping his work hours in proper perspective?

Major Decisions. Are there foreseeable changes in his life that should be considered, prayed about, and planned for now?

Obviously, each of these areas could command a complete article in its own right. But the questions I have listed help point to some of the most important concerns. A pastoral worker who was regularly addressing them would have some reason for confidence that he was helping the person grow in key areas of Christian life.

A few special notes. It is important to remember that the one-to-one pastoral relationship is meant to be a relationship of love, brotherhood, and service—not one of mere functionality. The goal is not to have a certain number of meetings and move through a checklist.

Second, the aim of one-to-one pastoral care is to help the individual take responsibility for his own growth and fruitfulness, not to assume responsibility for him. There are times when the pastoral leader should give authoritative direction. More often, he should *lead* the person into making his own decision in light of Scripture and the leading of the Spirit, augmented by the pastoral leader's input.

Finally, one-to-one pastoral care is a spiritual work, and can only be done well in a spiritual way. The pastoral worker should pray for the individual aside from their meetings, seek the Lord's mind and heart for him, and be prepared to share with him any word or insight the Lord may give. Obviously, opening and closing the pastoral appointment with prayer is always appropriate.

We can also understand what one-to-one pastoral care is by contrasting it with some other, more familiar, models of pastoral care.

Perhaps most of us, when we think of one-to-one pastoral care, think first of pastoral *counseling*. This can take many forms: marriage counseling, psychological counseling, drug counseling, and so on. Counseling is an indispensible pastoral tool. But it differs from the kind of one-to-one care I am describing in several important respects:

• Counseling is based on the felt need of the person being counseled. He (or she) takes the initiative to seek counseling if and when he feels the need for it. He decides which areas of life he will seek counseling for. In short, he sets the agenda.

• The counseling process is problem-driven. It has its origins in a perceived problem, and its only goal is to address that problem. Counseling ends when the problem is solved (or is declared insoluble).

• Counseling uses a "client" approach modeled on the helping professions. One party dispenses a service, the other party receives (and perhaps pays for) that service. There may be no other contact between the two parties whatsoever.

- Finally, in a counseling relationship the client may or may not follow the advice he is given. He can "shop around" for the advice he likes best. If at any point he does not like the advice he is getting, he can simply walk away.

Many pastoral leaders who rely exclusively on counseling as their only mode of one-to-one pastoral care find themselves drowning in a sea of problems, which they are trying to solve with one hand tied behind their backs.

The kind of one-to-one pastoral care I am writing about can be distinguished from counseling in each of the areas I have outlined:

- In one-to-one pastoral care the pastor takes the initiative and oversees the agenda, though the process is certainly influenced by the need and input of the individual.

- Instead of being problem-driven, the process is growth-oriented. The goal is not just to resolve a particular difficulty, but to help an individual grow in maturity, character, dedication, competence.

- Whereas counseling tends to be a somewhat impersonal (even mercantile) transaction, one-to-one pastoral care is founded on a personal relationship of love and trust. The pastoral leader and the individual under his care know, and are known by, each other. They think of one another primarily as brothers in the Lord.

- Finally, one-to-one pastoral care assumes some level of commitment and involves some degree of authority and subordination. The two parties are involved in the process not simply by mutual consent but because they see it as an expression of God's order for pastoral leadership in the church.

A System of Care

But who can provide it?

I suspect by now it is clear that in most cases the "someone" is not going to be the pastor of the church or the main leader of the community or group. No matter how capable he is, there are too many others for him to lead. Where does that leave us?

I believe it leaves us with a need for a *system* by which pastoral care in our churches, communities, and groups is exercised by *auxiliary* pastoral workers, on behalf of the main leadership, to provide personalized care.

I would now like to present the broad outlines of such a system of one-to-one pastoral care. I want to be clear at the outset that my goal is not to say, "This is the way; walk ye in it," but to say, "This is a good way; I highly recommend it." It is a *biblical* approach to pastoral care not in the sense that it follows a biblically mandated blueprint but in the sense that it presents an effective way to give expression to some important scriptural principles. It is also a *practical* approach, one that has proven its effectiveness in my own community and in numerous other groups where it has been used.

Scripture provides us with several insights into the need for a system of pastoral care and how it might be constructed. One is found in the encounter between Moses and his father-in-law, Jethro, recorded in Exodus 18.

Moses by this time has quite a burgeoning congregation on his hands, and he is beginning to sag under a burden of responsibility that sounds quite familiar to over-worked pastoral leaders in our day. "The next day Moses took his seat to serve as judge for the people, and they stood around him from morning till evening" (Ex 18:13).

Jethro immediately notices the problem and suggests a remedy.

"Select capable men from all the people—men who fear God, trustworthy men who hate dishonest gain—and appoint them as officials over thousands, hundreds, fifties, and tens. Have them serve as judges for the people at all times, but have them bring every difficult case to you; the simple cases they can decide themselves. That will make your load lighter because they will share it with you. If you do this and God so commands, you will be able to stand the strain, and all these people will go home satisfied" (Ex 18:21-23).

Note some things about Jethro's approach:

• Moses retains his overall authority, even as the brass-tacks work of pastoral care is handled "up close and personal" (the passage speaks of judges, but I believe it can refer more broadly to the entire realm of pastoral governance: it is the same word used in the Books of Judges and Samuel for those who ruled Israel before the monarchy).

• The solution is essentially pragmatic in nature: there is a concrete need, and this is a concrete way to meet it.

• It is a solution that will benefit both Moses ("You will be able to stand the strain") and the congregation ("All these people will go home satisfied").

This kind of network of relationships, utilizing lay workers under a pastor's oversight, has proven its effectiveness in numerous settings down through the years. A prominent example is the "class system" devised by John Wesley to keep the fires of early Methodism burning hot. Here is how Wesley described the arrangements:

"That it may the more easily be discerned whether they [the rank-and-file members] are indeed working out their own salvation, each society is divided into smaller companies, called 'classes,' according to their respective places of abode. There are about 12 persons in a class, one of whom is styled the leader. It is his duty—

• "To see each person in his class once a week at least, in order (1) to inquire how his soul prospers; (2) to advise, reprove, comfort, or exhort, as occasion may require; (3) to receive what he is willing to give toward the relief of the preachers, church, and poor;

• "To meet the ministers and the stewards of the society once a week, in order (1) to inform the minister of any that are sick or of any that are disorderly and will not be reproved; (2) to pay the stewards what he has received of his class in the week preceding."

We see in Wesley's model the same characteristics that marked the system that Jethro proposed to Moses:

• The main leaders ("the ministers and stewards of the society") retain their overall responsibility and authority, while basic elements of pastoral care are handled by delegated workers on a day-to-day basis.

• Practical considerations are factored in (the classes are set up according to members' "respective places of abode").

• The end result is that the pastors can do their job more effectively and the people receive better care.

A Contemporary Model

The community in which I serve as a pastoral leader, The Word of God, has made effective use of one-to-one pastoral care during its 21-year history. I believe our approach is a helpful model for how a contemporary system of one-to-one pastoral care can be structured, both in renewal communities such as our own, and also in churches and other types of groupings.

Units of the community, called "districts," are led by pastoral leaders, called "coordinators." Key elements of the system:

• Each coordinator works with a team of men called "district heads," who help him lead and care for the people in the district. The coordinator provides one-to-one pastoral care for each of his district heads. That is, in addition to training them for their service and overseeing their work, he takes a concern for their personal well-being, their family life, and so on. This is the first link in the chain.

• Each district head cares for a group of families within the district. That is, he provides one-to-one pastoral care for a particular group of men. In some cases, one of these men may in turn be a pastoral worker responsible for yet another group of people. In other cases, the district head may not have a small group of his own, but oversees two or more pastoral workers who lead small groups.

The system can be expanded both "horizontally," by adding more district heads, and "vertically," by raising up additional subordinate pastoral workers as new people join the community.

In real life, of course, the system is more complex, including small groups for men and for women, care for singles, and so on. I have deliberately simplified things here so that the basic concept can be illustrated.

• Each member of the community identifies with a particular coordinator in terms of teaching and overall direction, yet has someone "within reach" for more regular contact, answering questions, solving problems, applying general teaching to specific circumstances, receiving appropriate personal direction and correction, and so on.

• Each coordinator, conversely, sees himself as responsible to lead, teach, and guide the entire group, but is able to extend his pastoral care to individuals in a more personal way via the district heads and other pastoral workers who serve under his direction.

What we are talking about, then, is multiplying our resources for leading Christians to maturity and for sustaining them in fruitful Christian living, by involving capable men and women in the church or group to give one-to-one pastoral care.

These are real pastoral leaders. They provide effective pastoral care and exercise genuine pastoral authority by delegation from the main leadership of the group. The scope of each one-to-one relationship, and of the pastoral authority appropriate to it, are clearly defined by the coordinator.

In The Word of God, we have all kinds of people providing one-to-one pastoral care for others: mechanics, accountants, college students, housewives. Some care for one or two people; others for six or eight or ten. Some serve for particular periods of time as needs arise, others have been "in harness" for many years and likely will continue to serve as pastoral workers indefinitely. All in all, perhaps as many as one-third of our adult members serve or have served in such a capacity.

Obviously, a crucial element in establishing a pastoral care system of this kind is identifying people who can take pastoral responsibility for others. This approach calls for a number of "middle-level" pastoral workers, serving under the main leaders' direction. Where do we find these people?

All around us! I believe most of our churches and groups have many people who, with appropriate orientation and training, would not only survive but thrive in roles of pastoral service. The main prerequisites are:

• **Having reached a level of basic maturity oneself.** You cannot lead people where you yourself have not gone.

• **Sound Christian character.** The third chapter of Paul's first letter to Timothy, and similar passages, demonstrate an emphasis on character over gift. Keep in mind that you are looking for "basic soundness" of character, not for perfection.

• **Good relational skills.** A pastoral worker functioning at this level needs to be a capable communicator and needs some basic aptitude for understanding "where people are at."

• **Commitment to the group.** You are looking for someone who can help others grow in the context of your particular church or community. The pastoral care role that I am describing is delegated from the main leadership and must be conducted with a willingness to be subordinate to that leadership. In other words, the kind of person you might choose for this role would be different from the kind of person you would select to launch a new church.

• **A servant's heart.** This, of course, is a basic prerequisite for *any* role of service among God's people.

In short, we are not looking for people who could replace us as overall leaders (praise God if we find some, though!). This is the mistake some of us make: we set the threshold so high that almost no one can cross it. We are simply looking for men and women who are "solid citizens" of the kingdom and who have a heart for helping others.

Where should a pastor begin? With himself. Think of a few men in the church with whom you would feel comfortable working in this way. Talk to them privately and explain what you have in mind (you might discuss this article together). Spend six months to a year "trying it on for size" with this group, working out the bugs, learning how to implement the basic approach in your particular situation. At this point, you are in effect modeling for this initial group how the process works.

As time goes on, suggest that the men you have been caring for enter into one-to-one pastoral relationships with other men in the church. It is usually inadvisable to "press the issue" prematurely— and often unnecessary to boot, as the good fruit that comes from this approach in the lives of those who participate in it is often the strongest point of attraction.

Notes

Chapter Eight

1. Peter Berger, *A Rumor of Angels*, p. 10.
2. As quoted in Berger, *Ibid*, p. 12.
3. Hans Kung, *On Being a Christian*, p. 28.
4. Harry Blamires, *The Christian Mind*, pp. 3, 37-38.
5. "Go . . . Liberate," NAE Resolution, 1986.
6. Vatican II, "Apostolicam Actuositatem," 18 November 1965("Decree on the Apostolate of Lay People").
7. Henry VanTil, *The Calvinistic Concept of Culture* (quote slightly amended), p. 25.
8. W. Breggeman, *The Prophetic Imagination*, p. 50.
9. Richard Mouw, *Called to Holy Worldliness*, pp. 33-67.
10. L.P. Gerlach and V.H. Hine, *People, Power, Change: Measurement of Social Transformation*, p. 110.
11. Marshal Baldwin, *The Middle Ages*, Vol III. p. 120.
12. See Kenneth S. Latourette, *A History of Expansion of Christianity*, Volume II; Marshal Baldwin, *The Middle Ages*, Volume III.
13. Quoted by David L. Watson, *Accountable Discipleship*, p. 84.
14. *Directory for Private Social Worship 1801*, Reformed Presbyterian Church, Scotland, p. 6.
15. Ibid, p. 7.
16. Ibid, p. 46.
17. Ibid, p. 52.
18. Ibid, p. 53.
19. Earnest House, *Saints in Politics*, p. 25.
20. Ibid, p. 25.
21. Ibid, p. 30.
22. David L. Edwards, *Christian England*, Vol. 3, p. 87.
23. David McAllister, *The National Reform Association*, pp. 106-182.
24. See Gary Smith, *The Seeds of Secularism, Calvinism, Culture, Pluralism*.
25. Frank VanderBerg, *Abram Kuyper*, p. 100.
26. Ibid, p. 101.
27. As quoted by George Marsden in Shipps and Carpenter, *Making Higher Education Christian*, p. 51.

Chapter Nine

1. A slightly different version of this material appeared in *Truth,* Vol. 1, 1985.
2. New York: Macmillan, 1980.
3. W.E. Graddy, *New Oxford Review,* June 1982.
4. New York: Macmillan, 1976.
5. J.E Gedo and G.H. Pollock, editors, *Freud: The Fusion of Science and Humanism* (New York: International University, 1967).
6. Sigmund Freud and Oskar Pfister, *Psychoanalysis and Faith* (New York: Basic Books, 1963), p. 117.
7. See Freud, *The Ego and the Id* (New York: Norton, 1923/1962), pps. 26-28; p. 33.
8. For a detailed development of this position see P. Vitz, *Sigmund Freud's Christian Unconscious* (New York: Guilford, 1988).
9. Freud, 1919, Standard Edition, 17, p. 193; also 1905, S.E.,7, p. 226ff; 1909, S.E., 11, p. 47.
10. From *Le neveau de Rameau*; quoted by Freud in Lecture XXI of his Introductory Lectures (1916-1917), S.E., 16, pp. 331-338.
11. *Leonardo da Vinci*, 1910, 1947 p. 98.
12. For the supporting biographical material on Freud see, for example, M. Krull, *Freud und sein Vater,* (Munich: Beck, 1979), and Vitz, *Sigmund Freud's Christian Unconscious* (New York: Guilford, 1988).
13. W.J. Murray, *My Life without God* (Nashville, Tenn.: Nelson, 1982).
14. See page 11.
15. *Growing Up* (New York: Congdon and Weed, 1982).

Allies for Faith and Renewal Conferences, Tapes, and Books

Allies for Faith and Renewal conferences are held annually by the Center for Pastoral Renewal and are open to all Christians who share the purposes of the conferences stated on page 15. To receive information about the next conference, write to the Center at the address below.

Books of previous Allies conferences are also available:

Christianity Confronts Modernity (1980 conference)
Summons to Faith and Renewal (1982)
Christianity in Conflict (1985)
Christian Allies in a Secular Age (1986)
Courage in Leadership (1987)

A set of all four volumes costs $32.00. Individual volumes, including the present book, are $7.95 each. When ordering, please enclose an additional 10 percent to cover handling and postage (20 percent outside the United States and Canada). Payment must accompany order.

Audio cassettes of many Allies conference presentations are also available. An order list may be obtained from the Center for Pastoral Renewal.

Pastoral Renewal

The bimonthly publication of the Center for Pastoral Renewal offers analysis of pastoral issues, practical issues, practical pastoral, and personal encouragement to clergy and lay leaders in Protestant, Roman Catholic, and Orthodox churches and fellowships. To receive a sample issue write to the Center for Pastoral Renewal.

The Center for Pastoral Renewal
Department AKW
P.O. Box 8617
Ann Arbor, MI 48107
(313) 761-8505